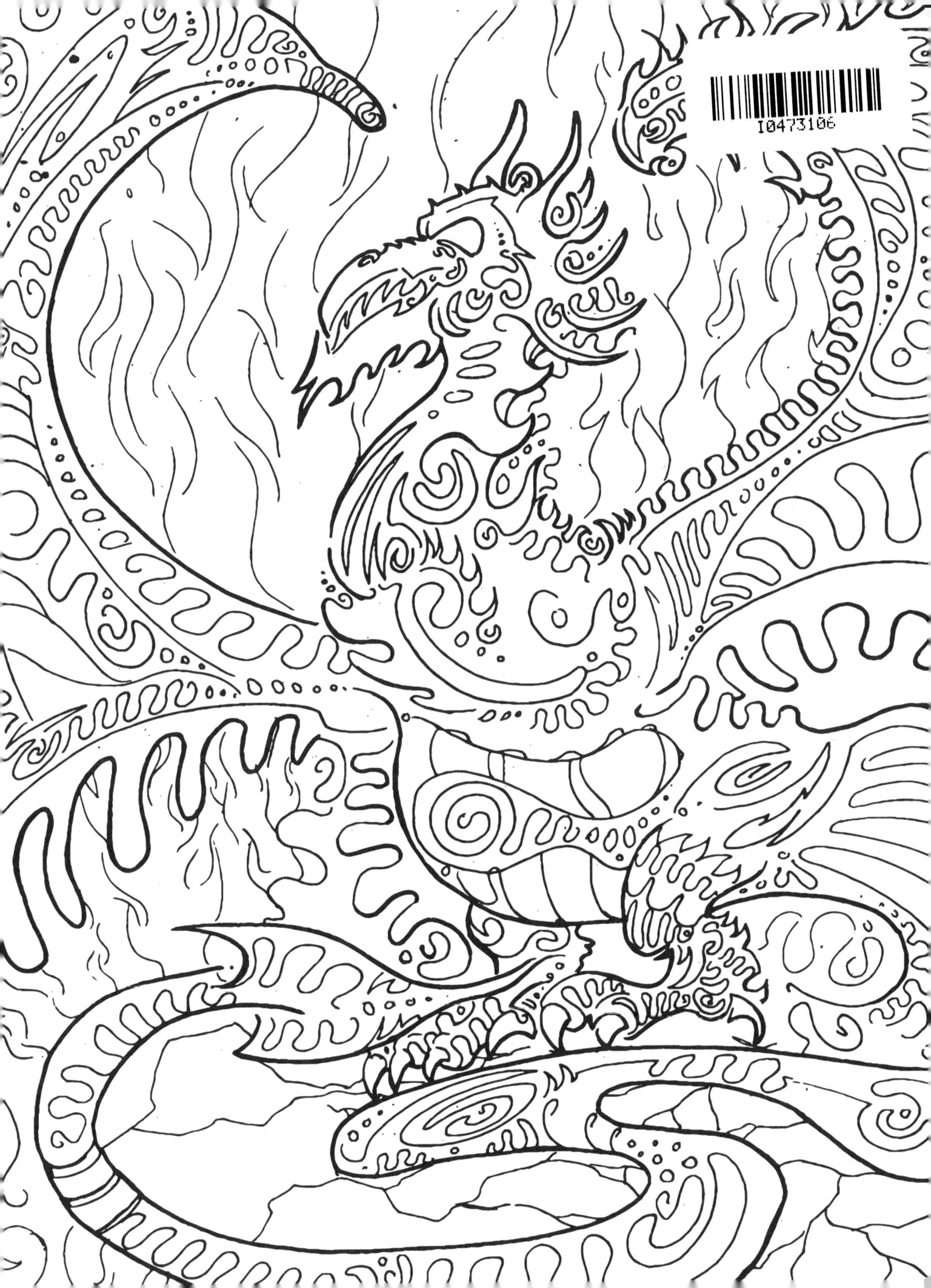

This page was left intentionally blank

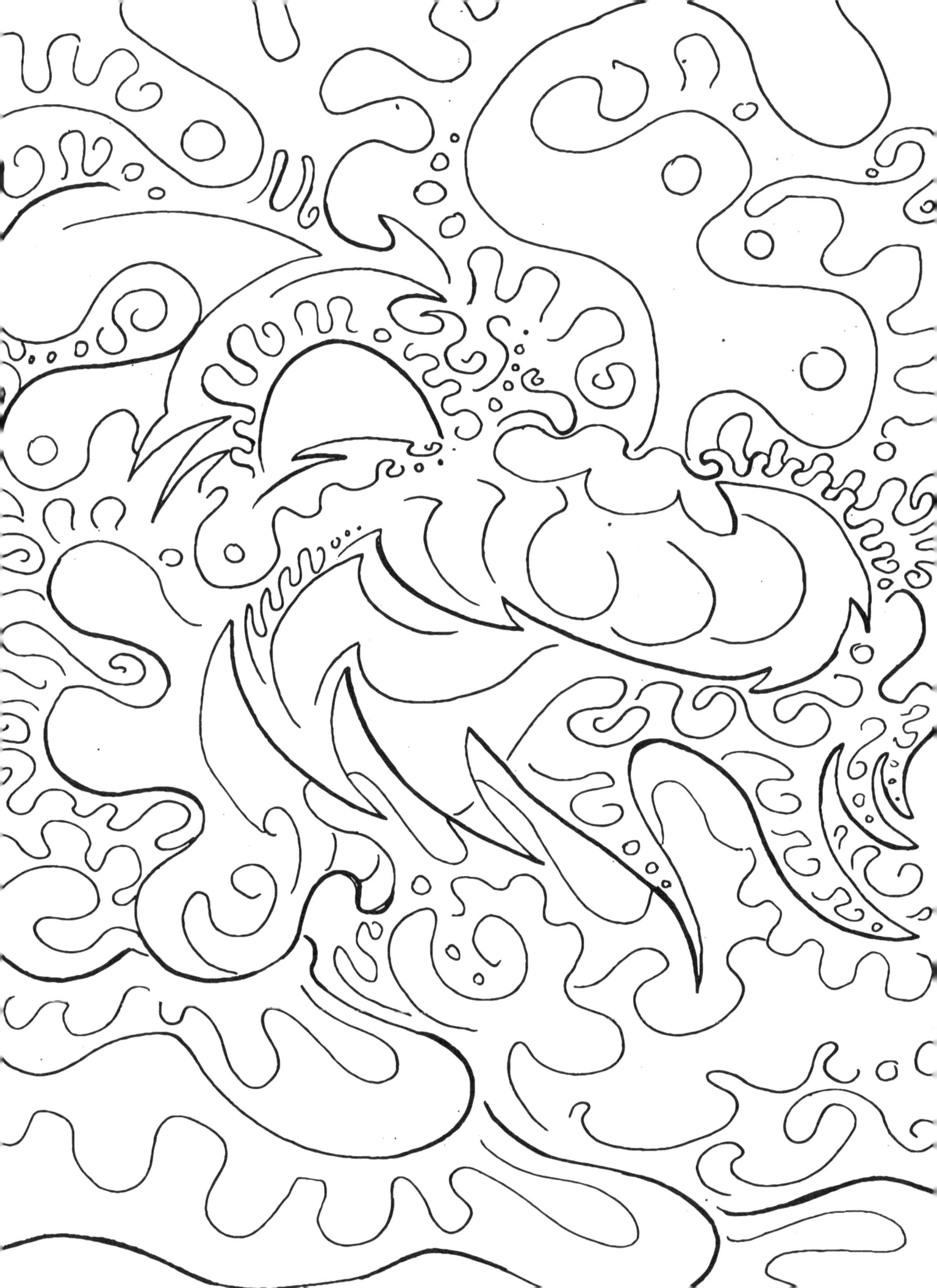

This page was left intentionally blank

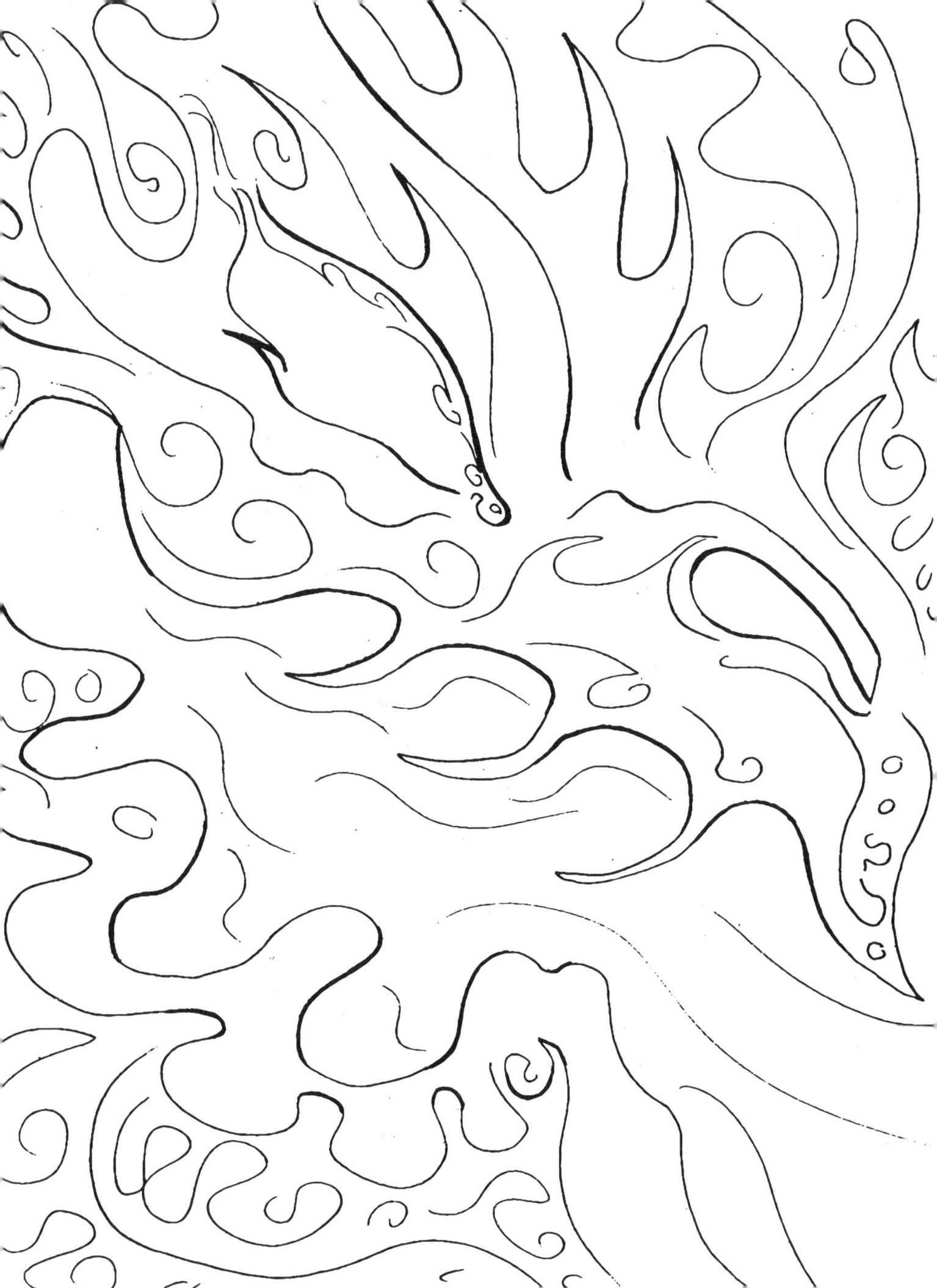

This page was left intentionally blank

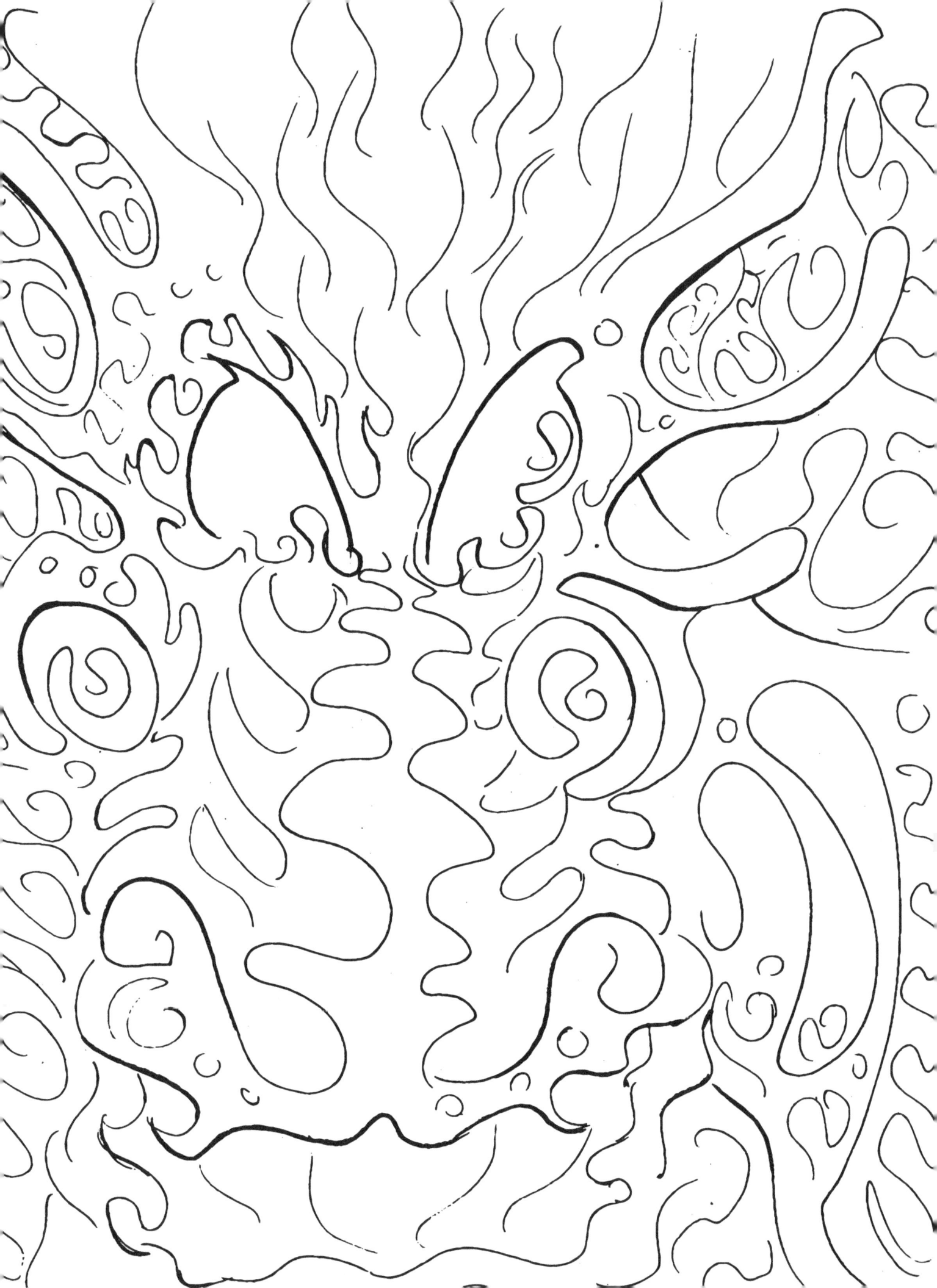

This page was left intentionally blank

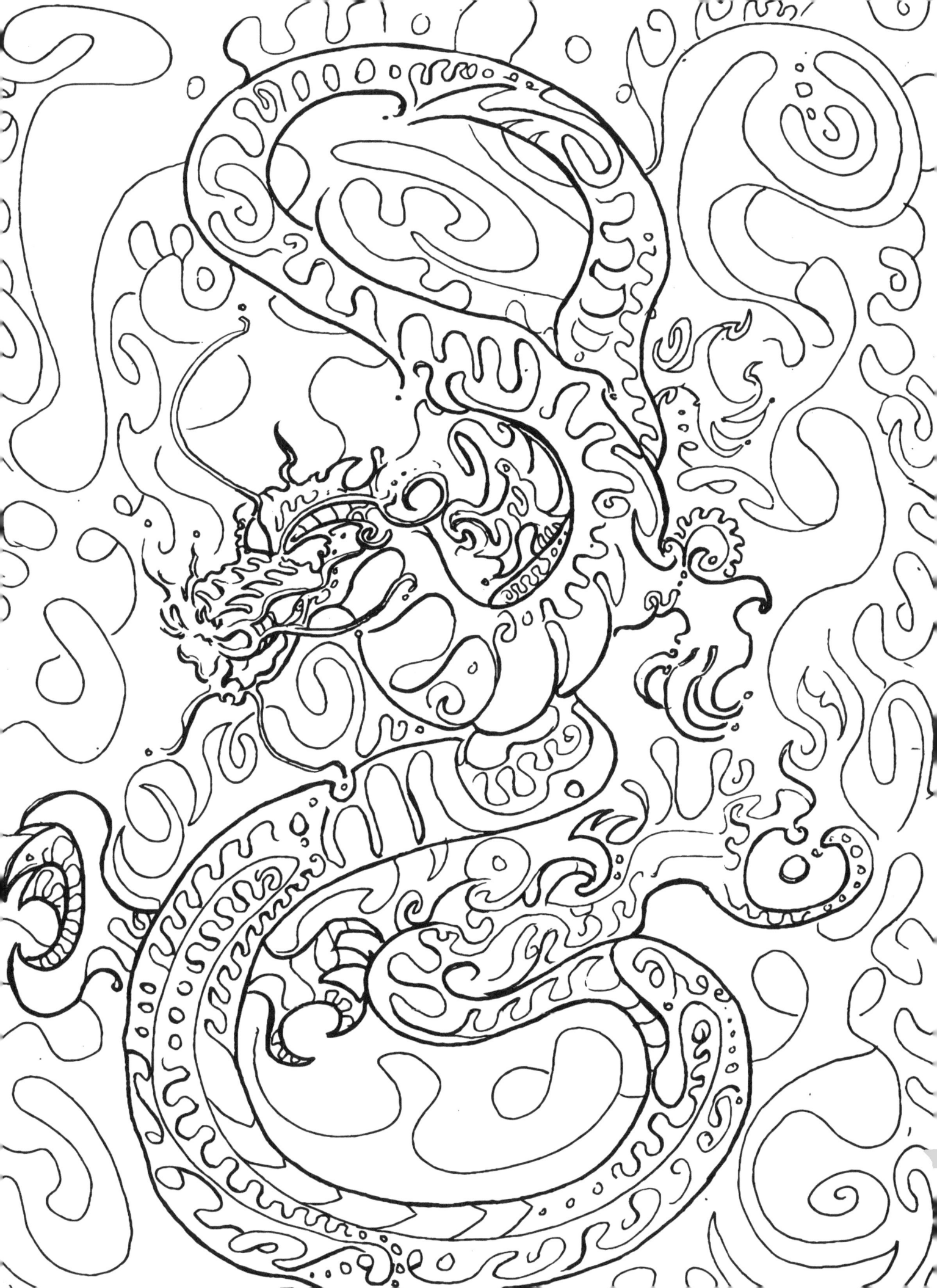

This page was left intentionally blank

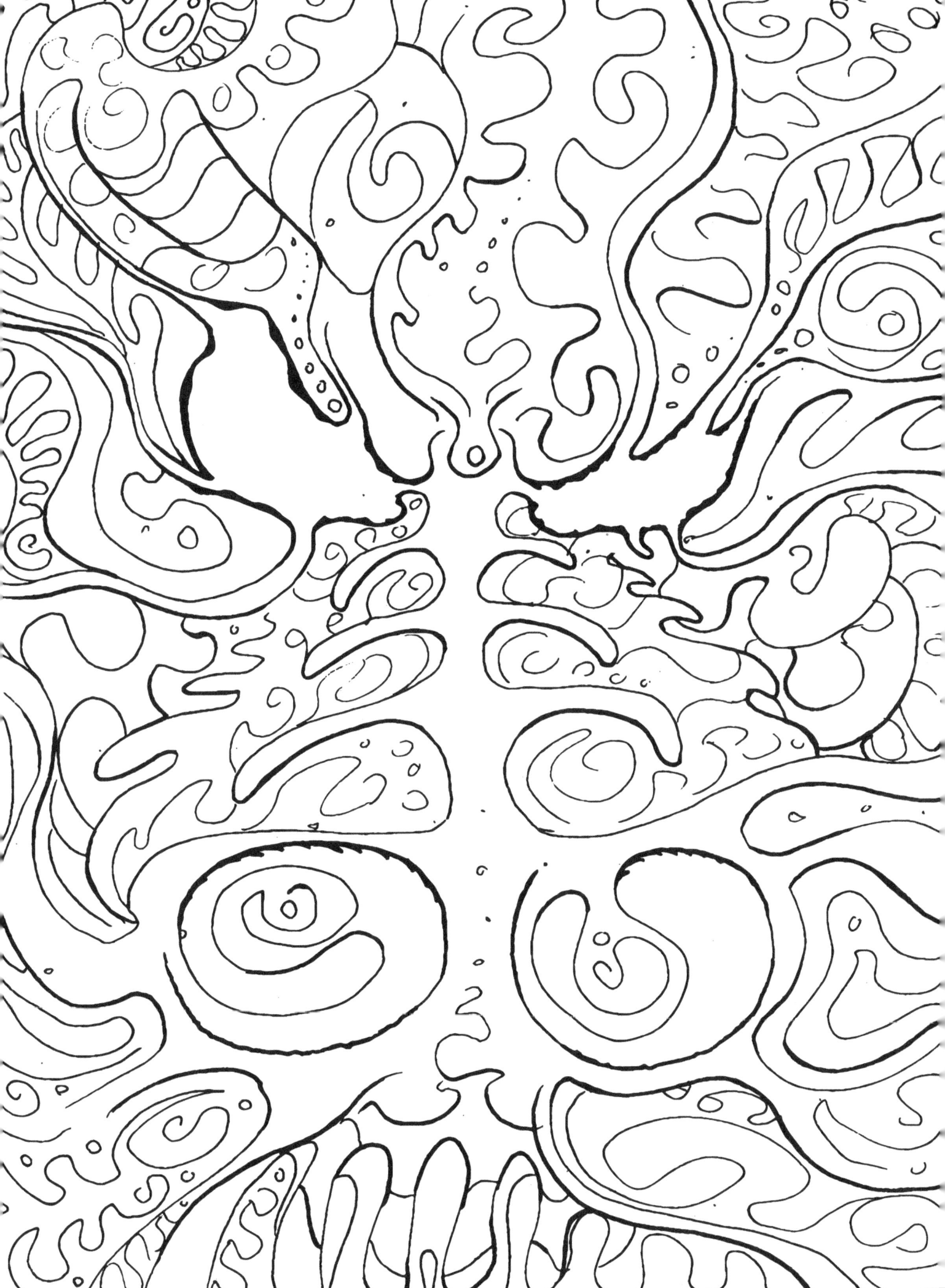

This page was left intentionally blank

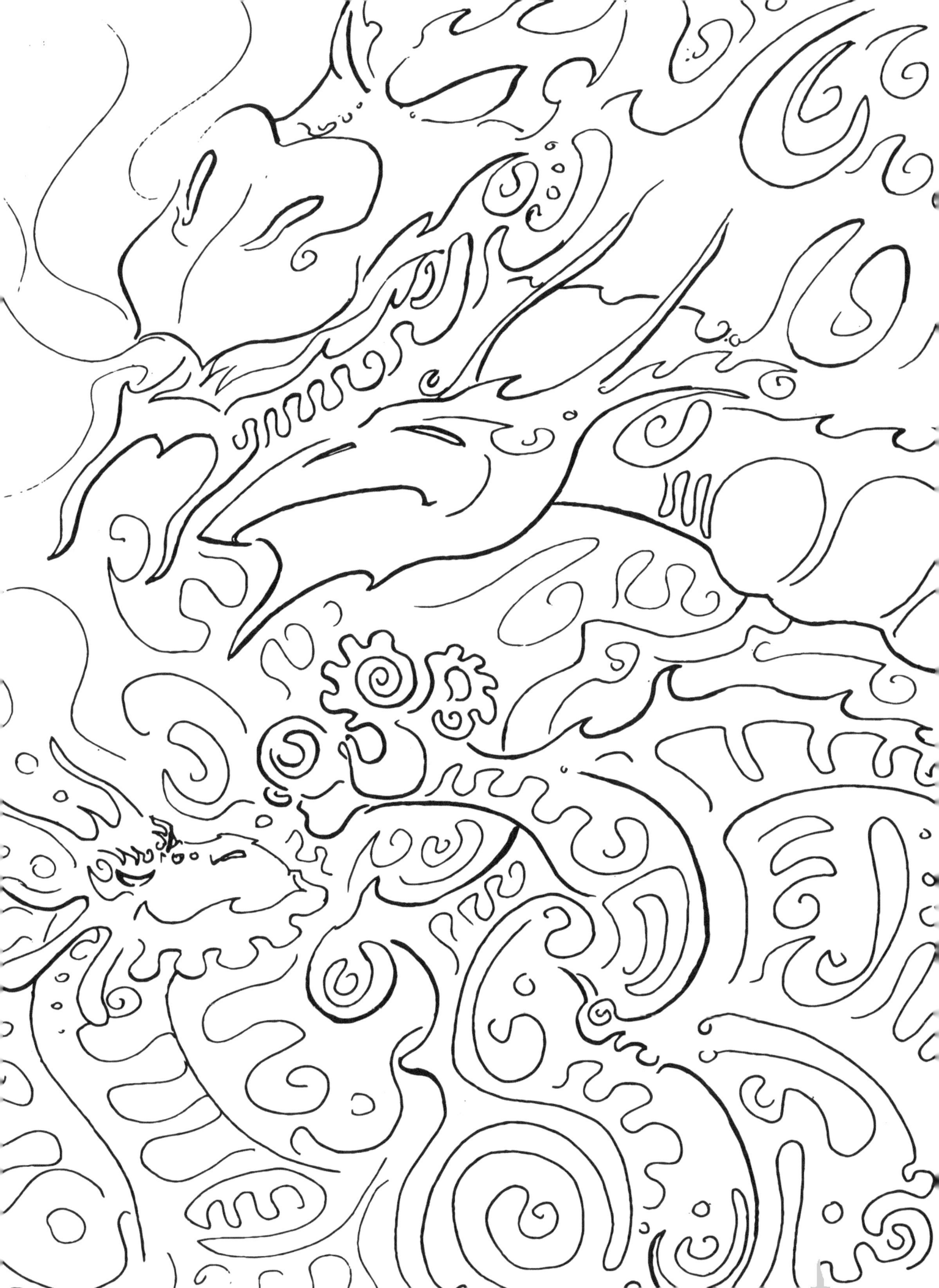

This page was left intentionally blank

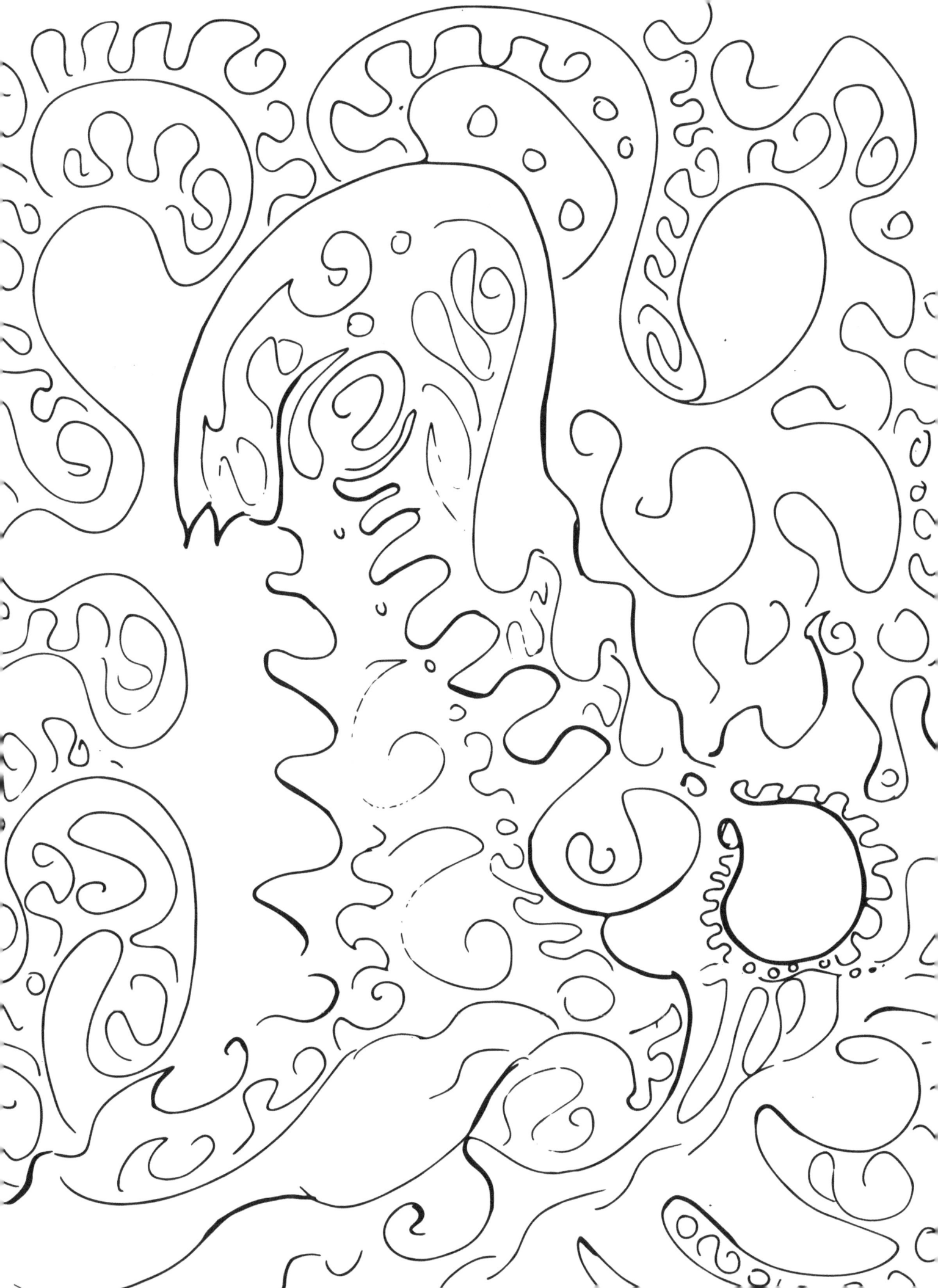

This page was left intentionally blank

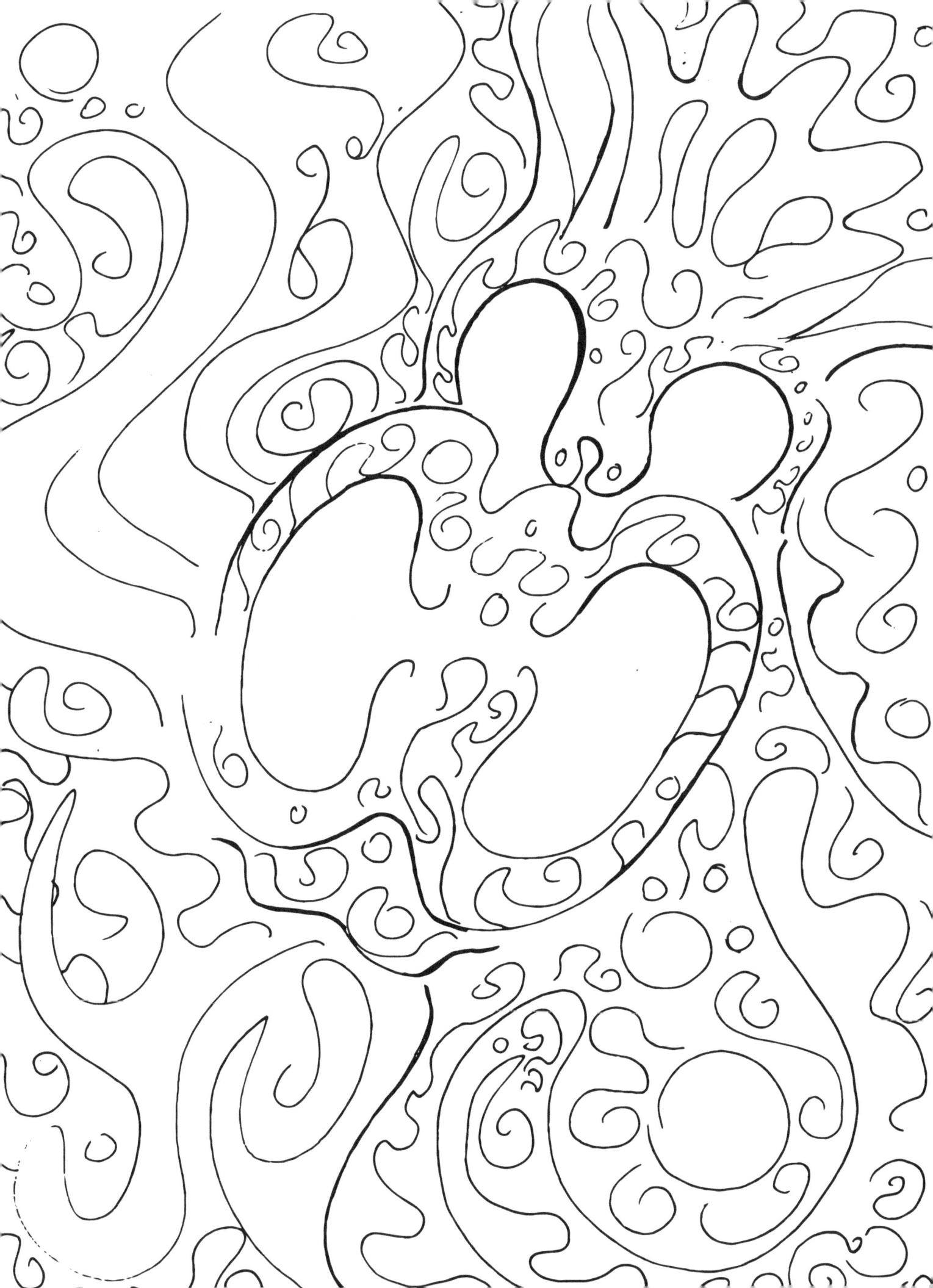

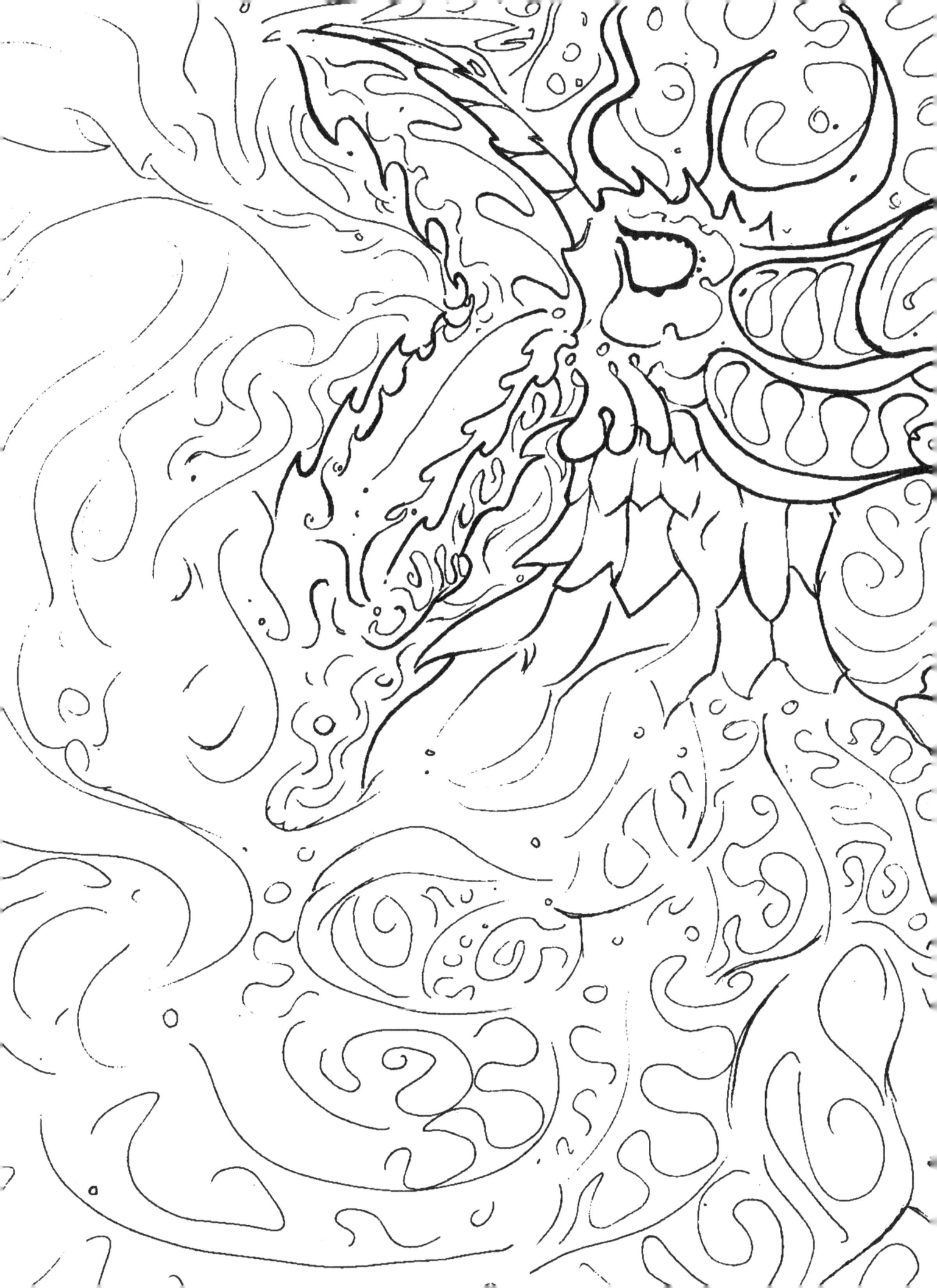

This page was left intentionally blank

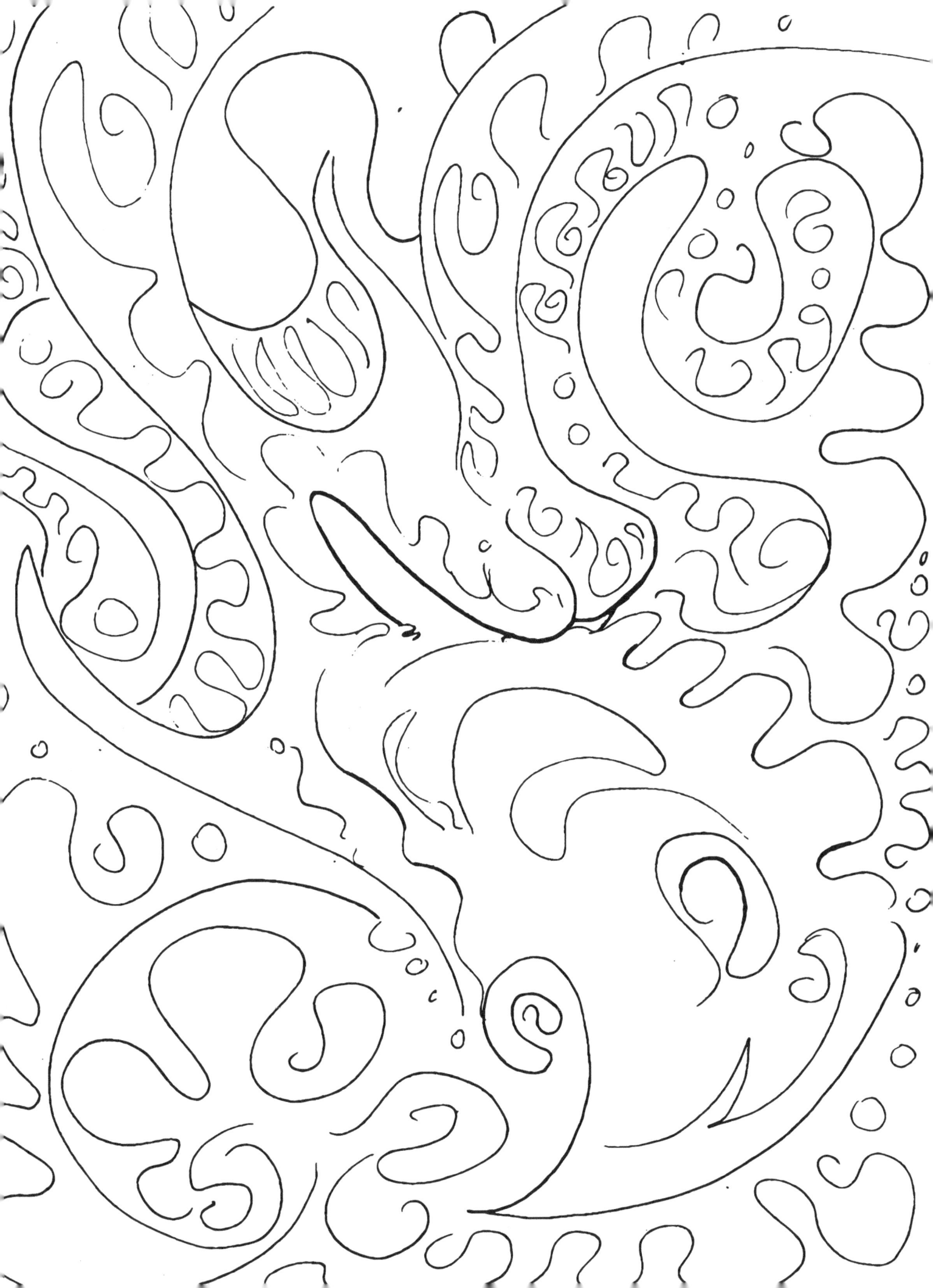

This page was left intentionally blank

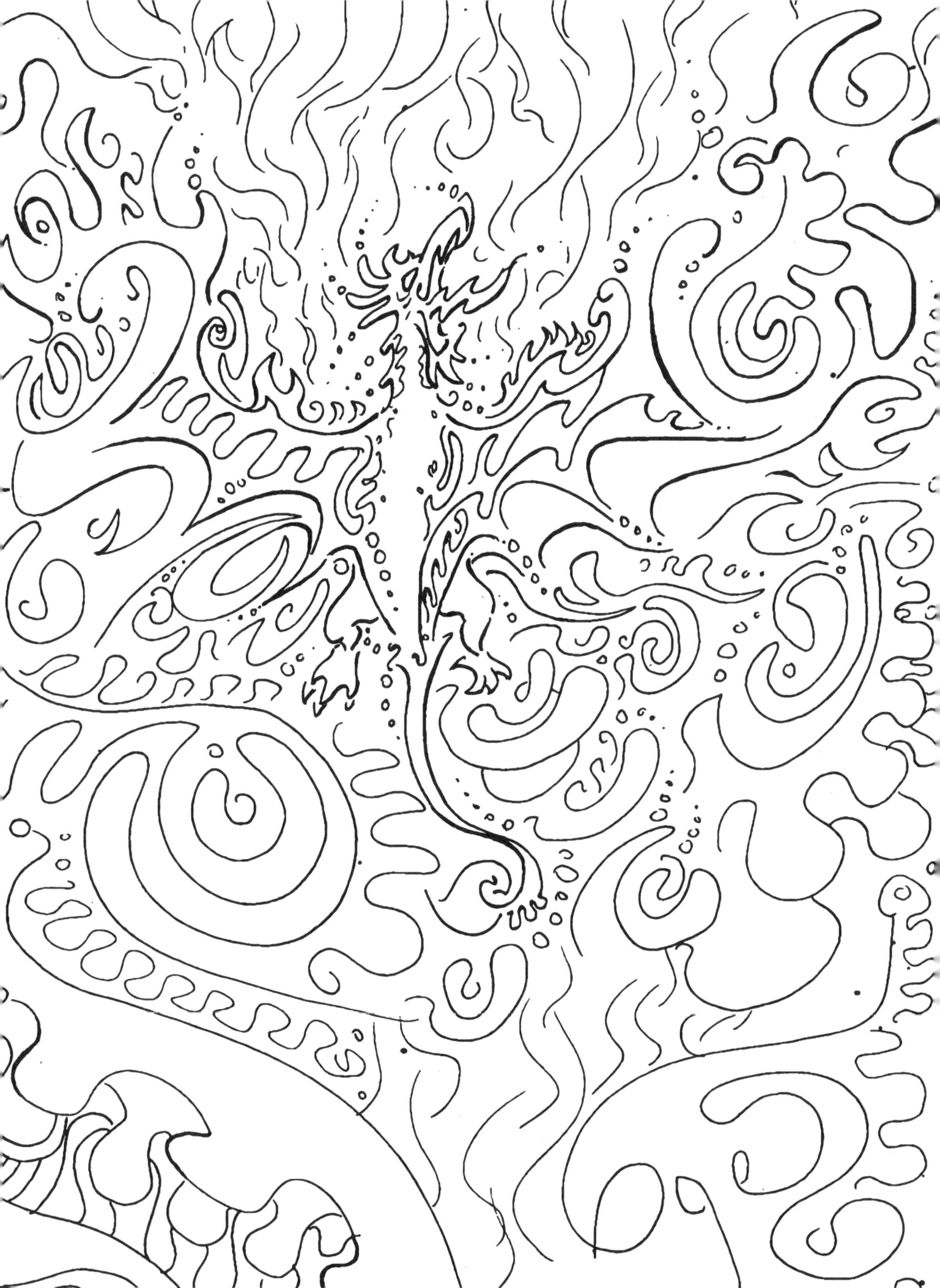

This page was left intentionally blank

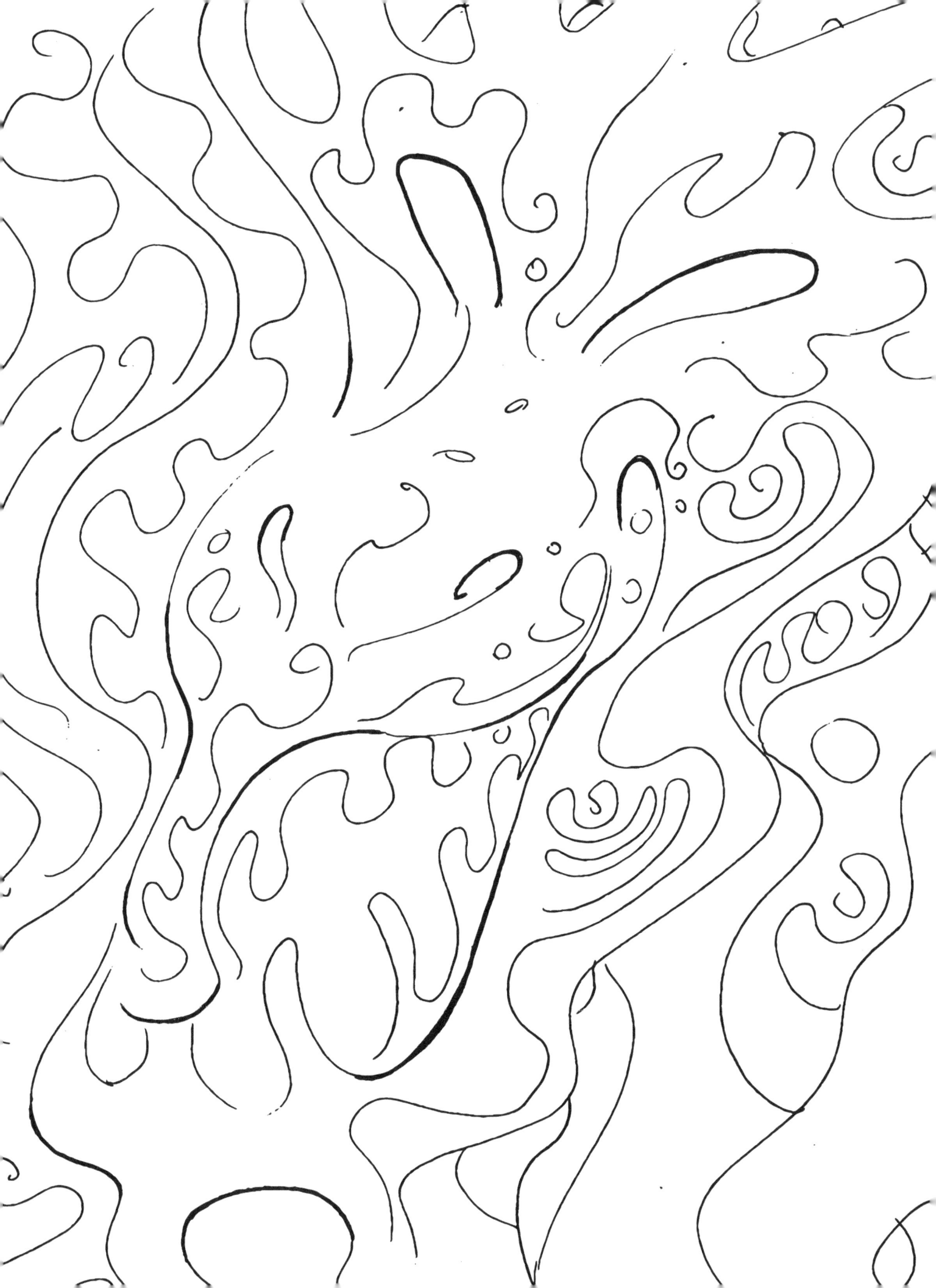

This page was left intentionally blank

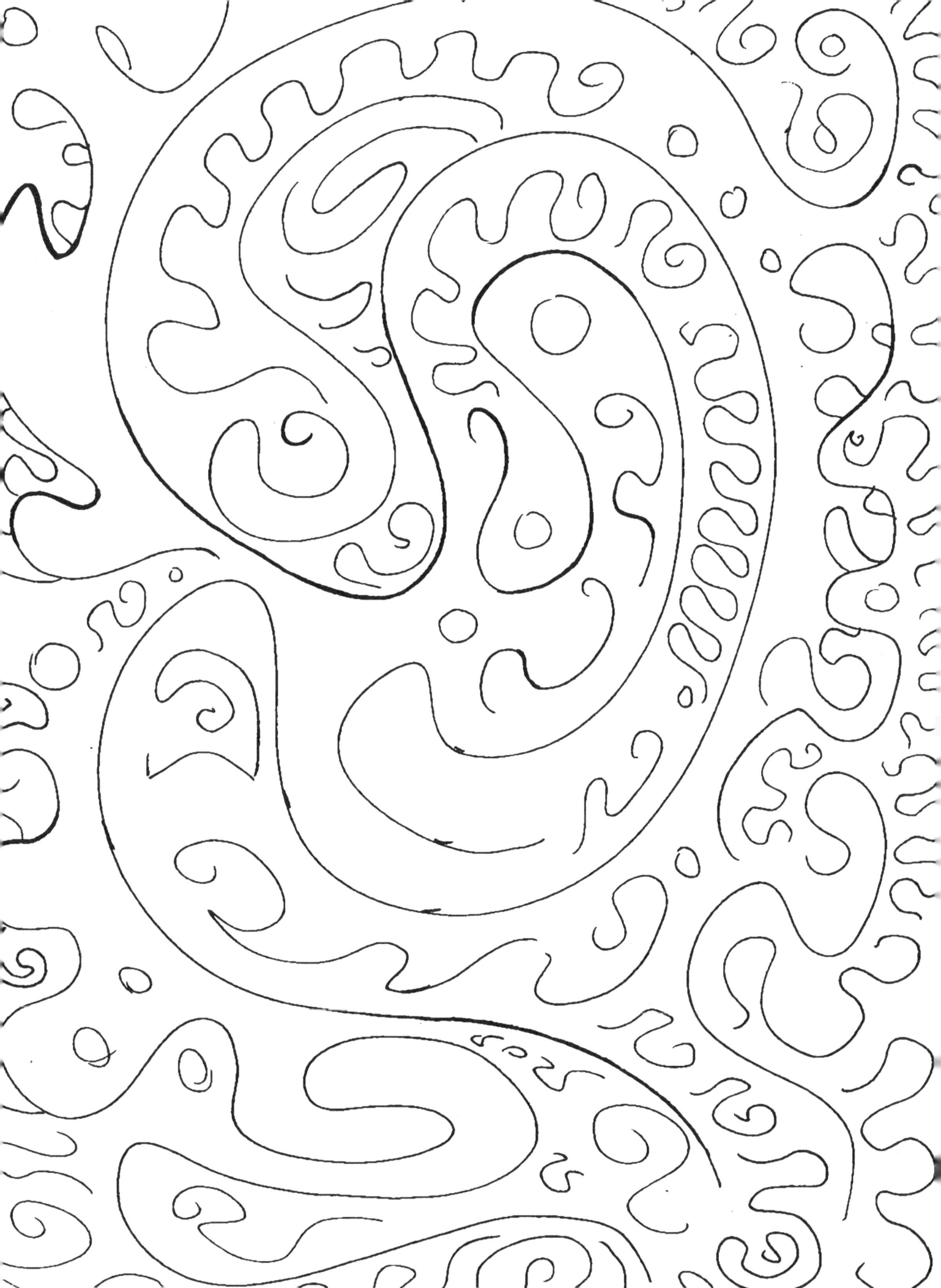

This page was left intentionally blank

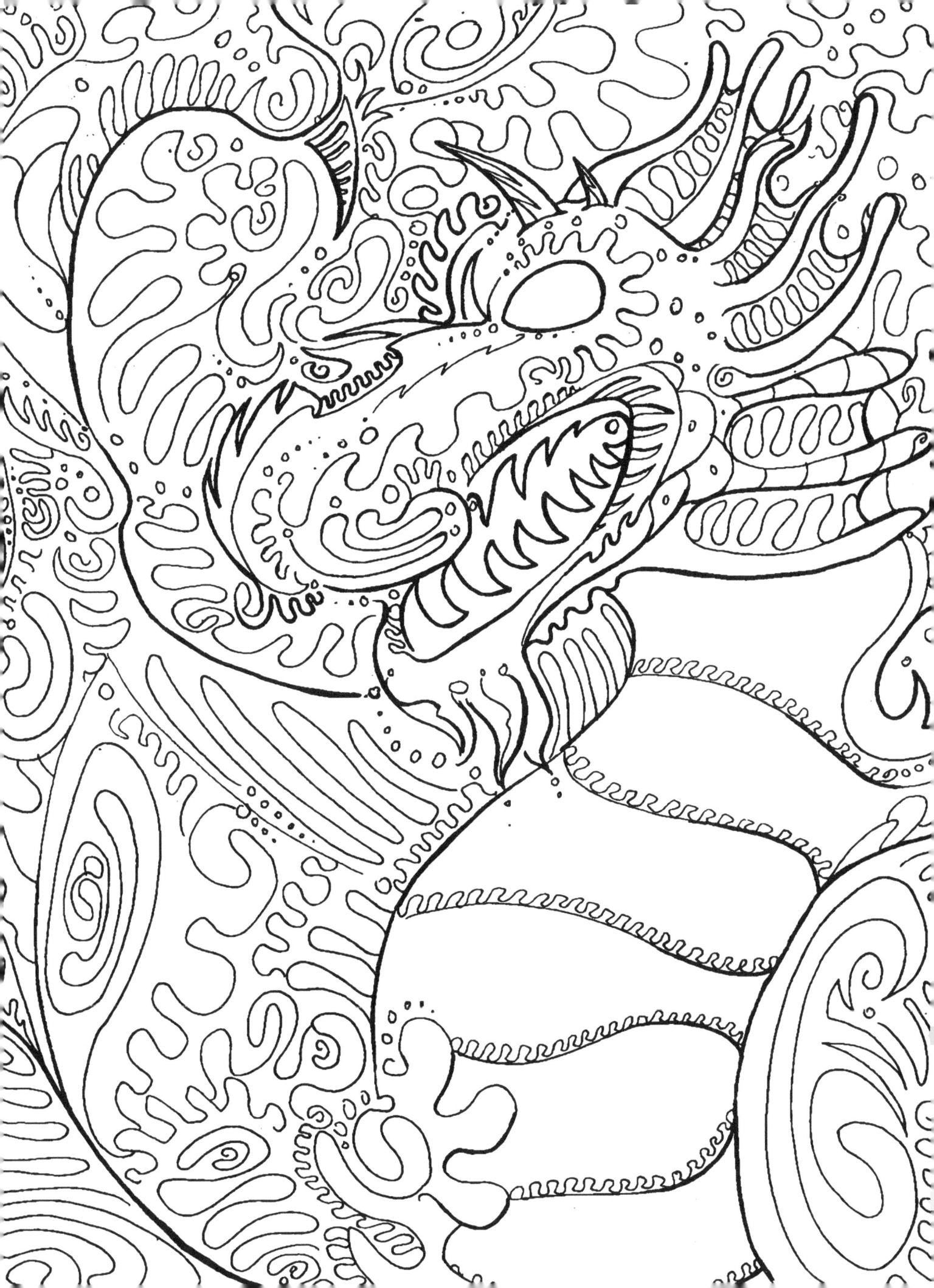

This page was left intentionally blank

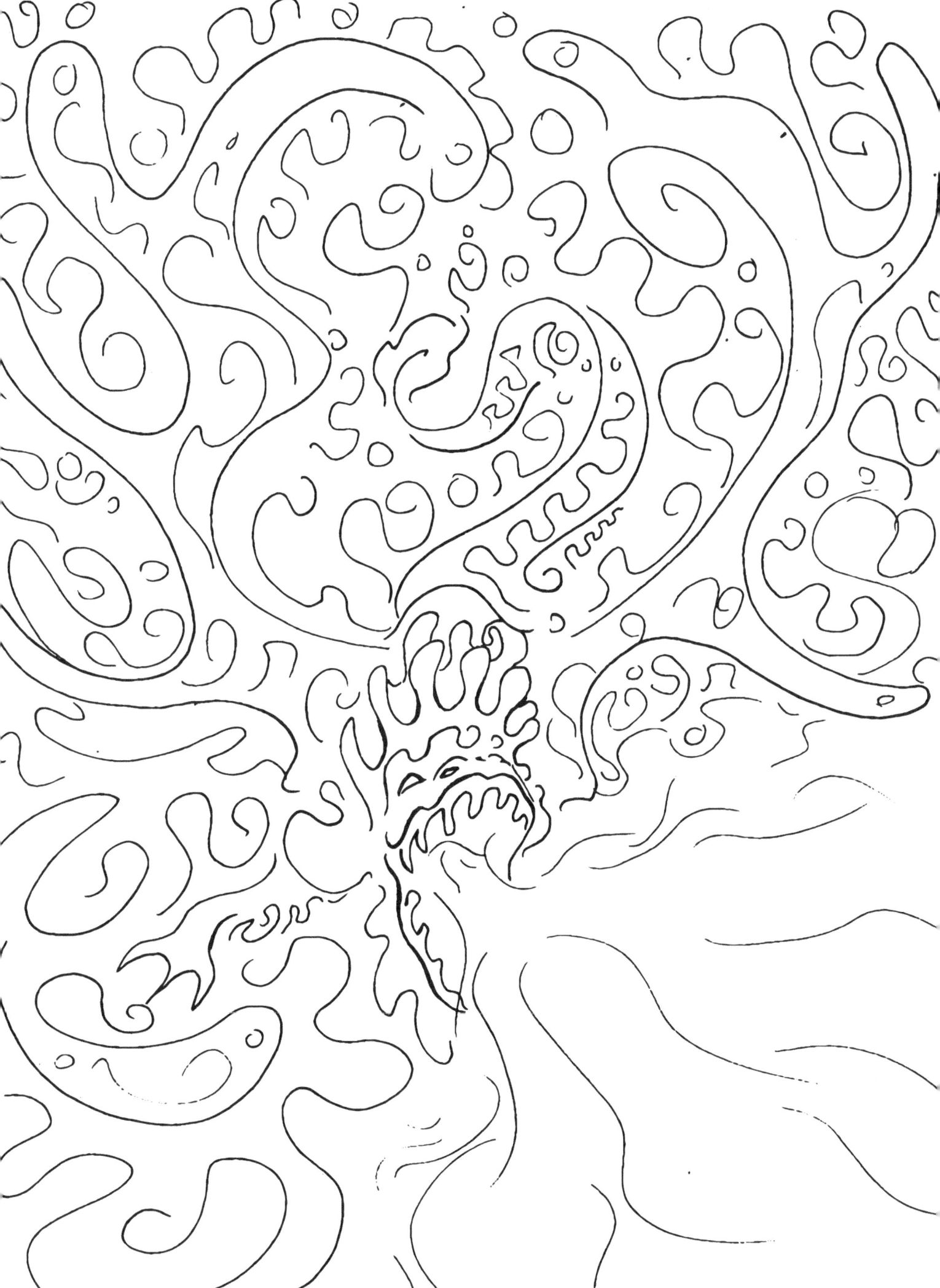

This page was left intentionally blank

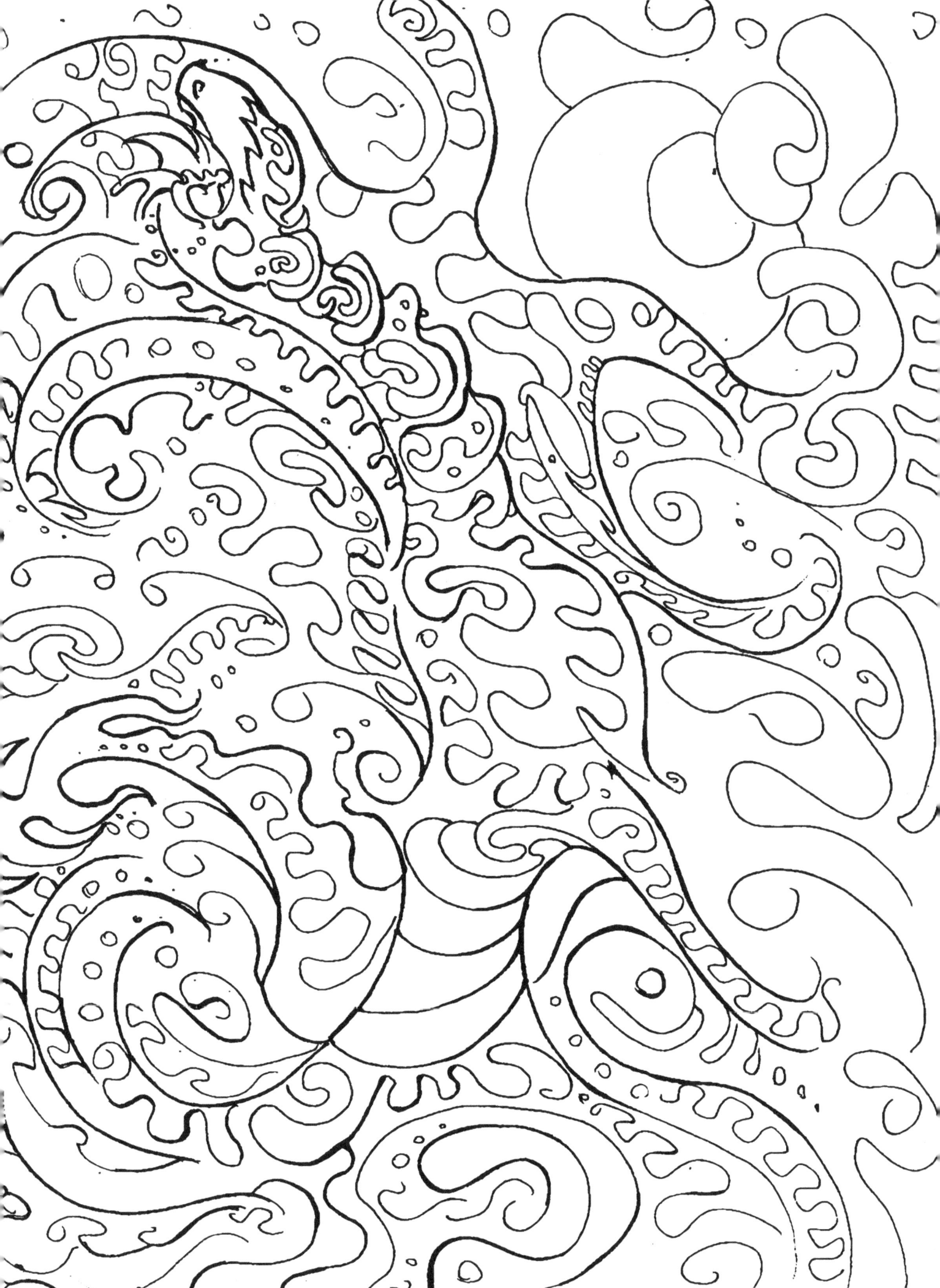

This page was left intentionally blank

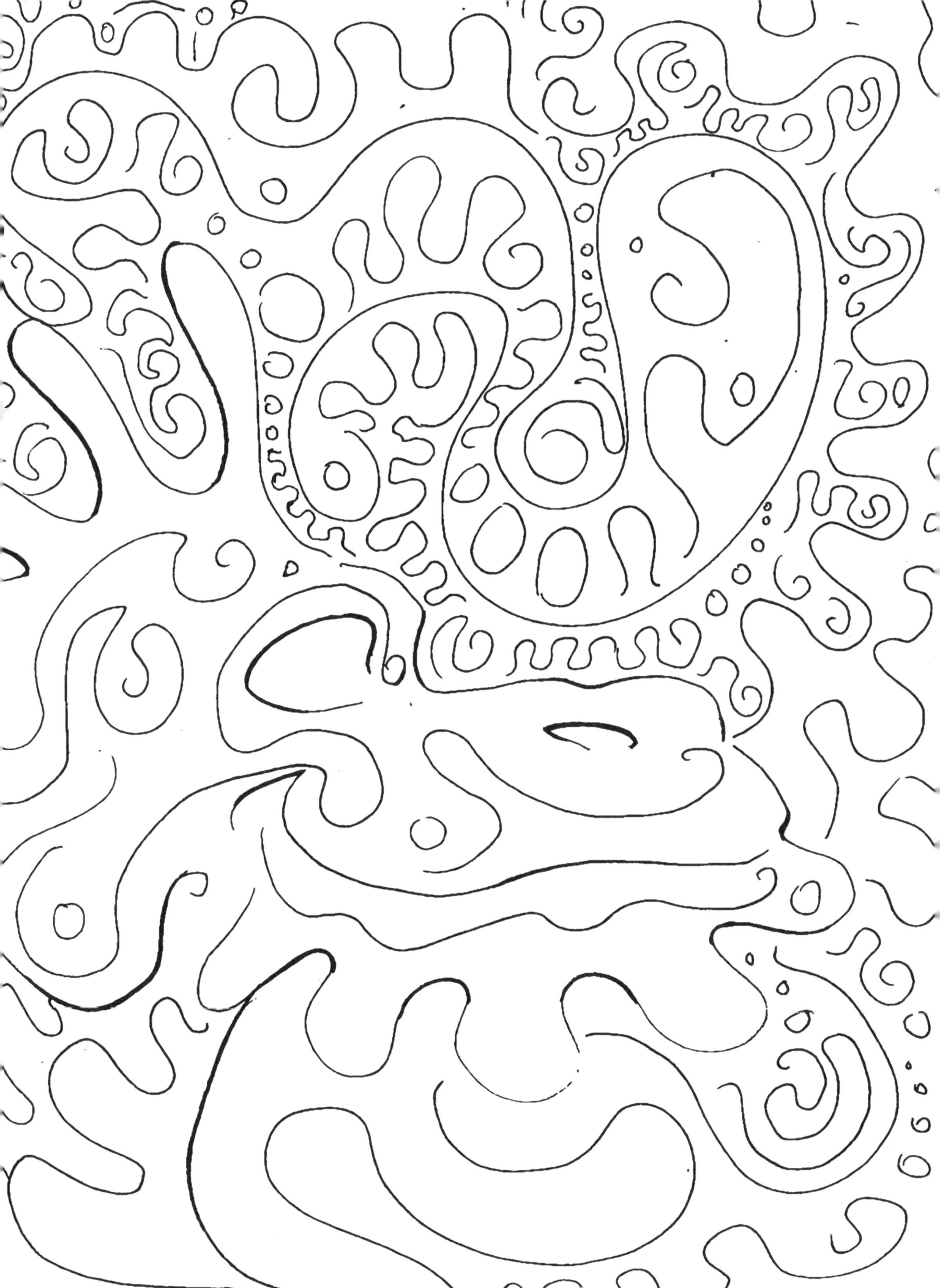

This page was left intentionally blank

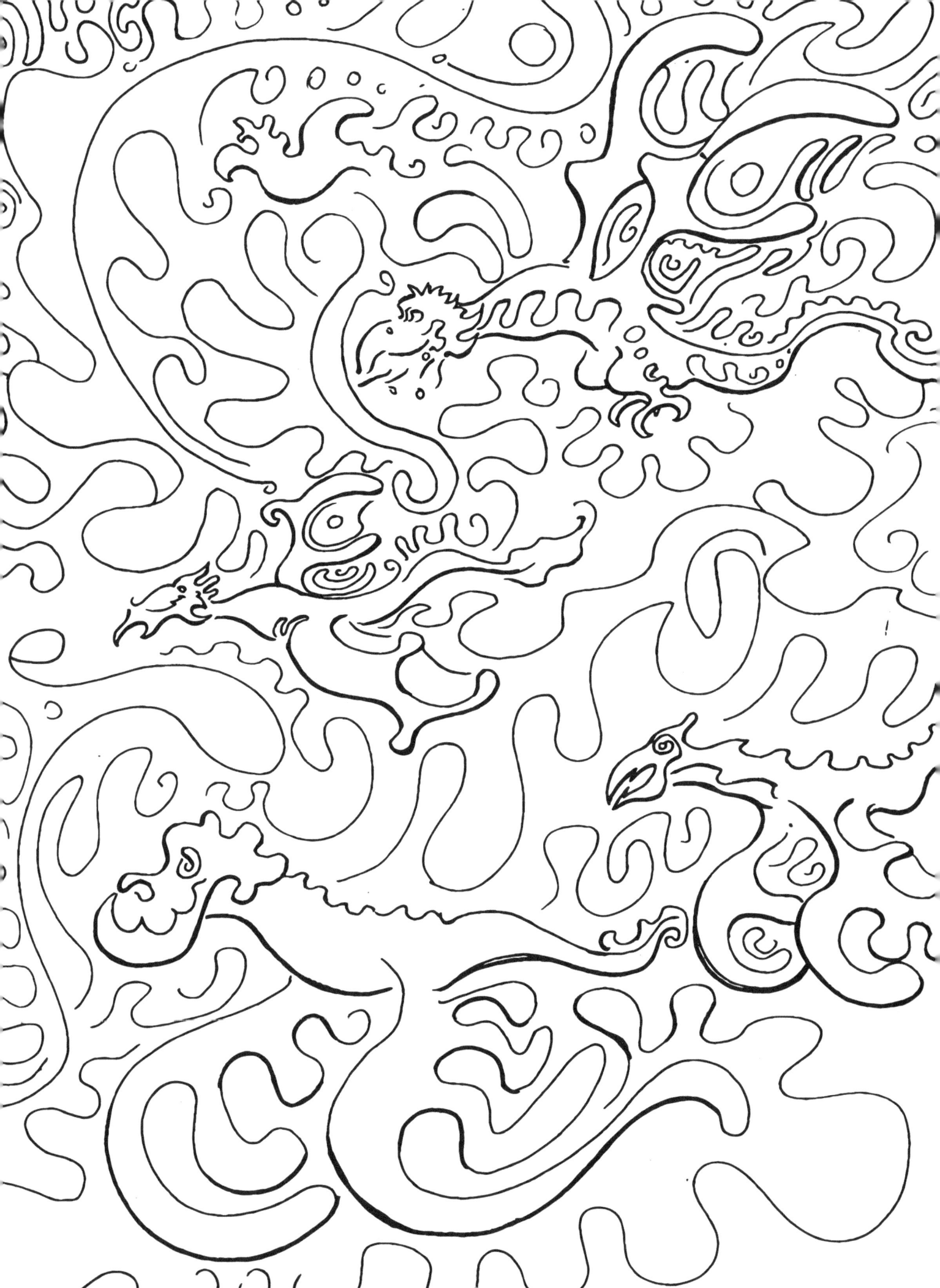

This page was left intentionally blank

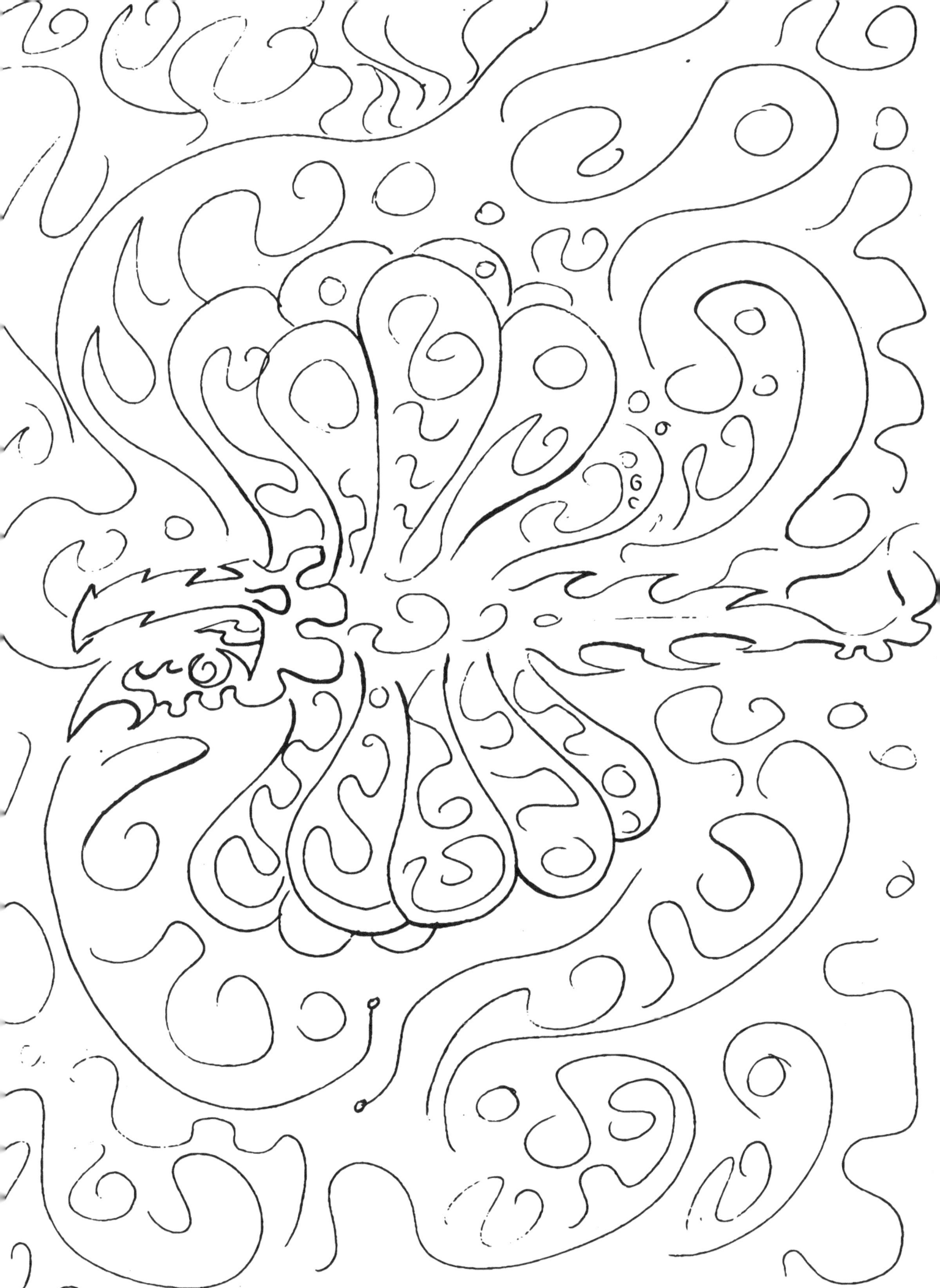

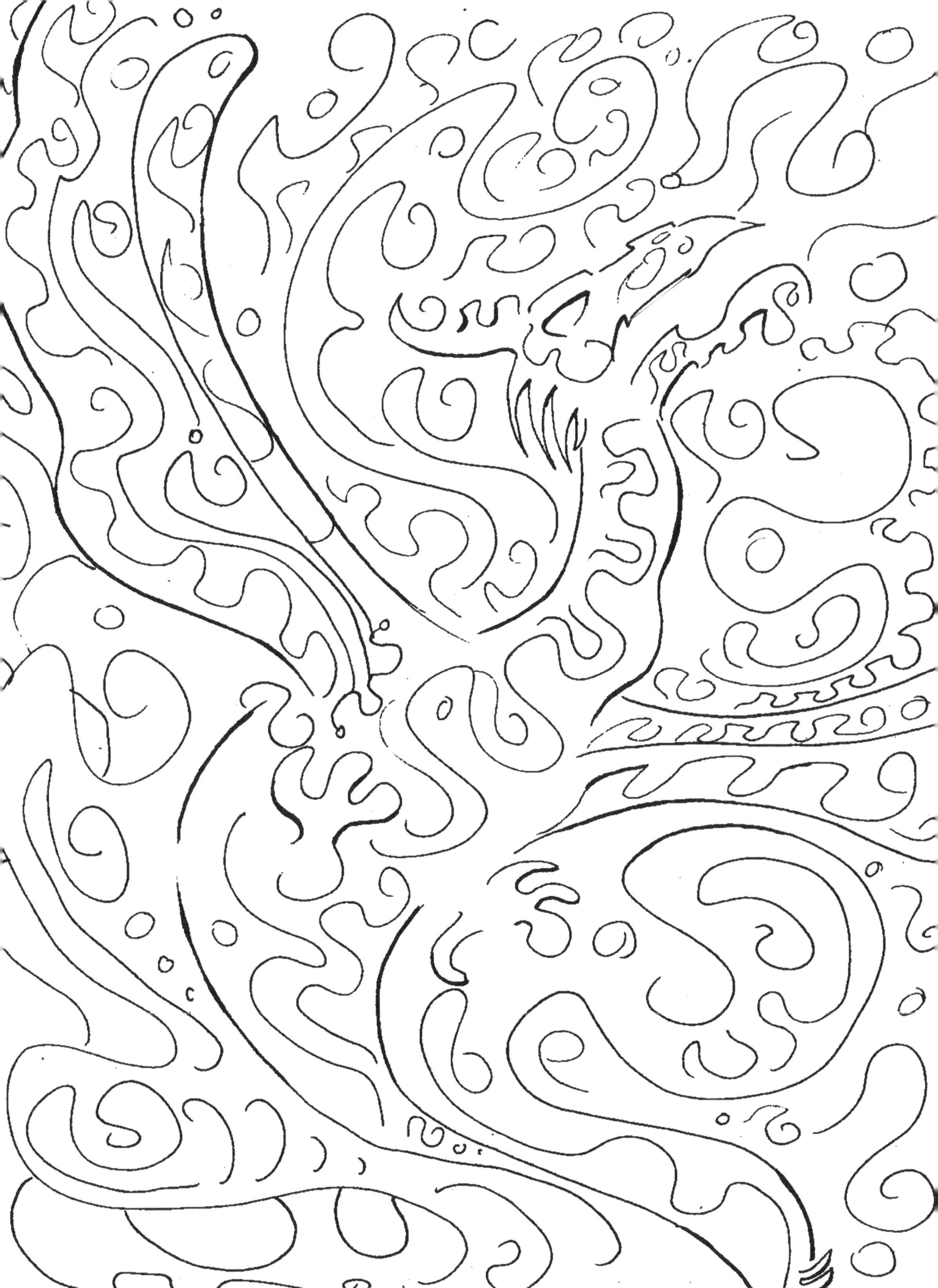

This page was left intentionally blank

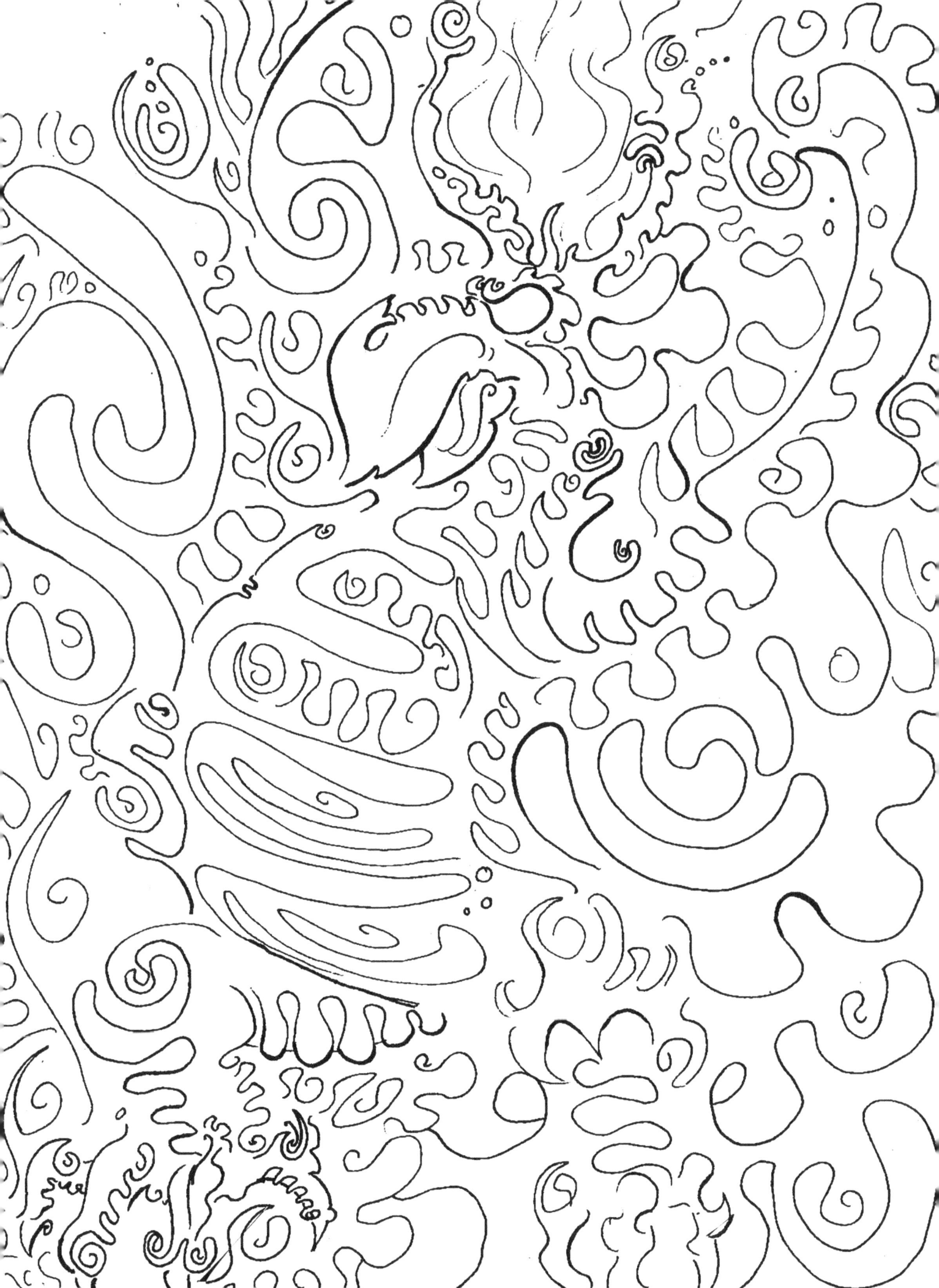

This page was left intentionally blank

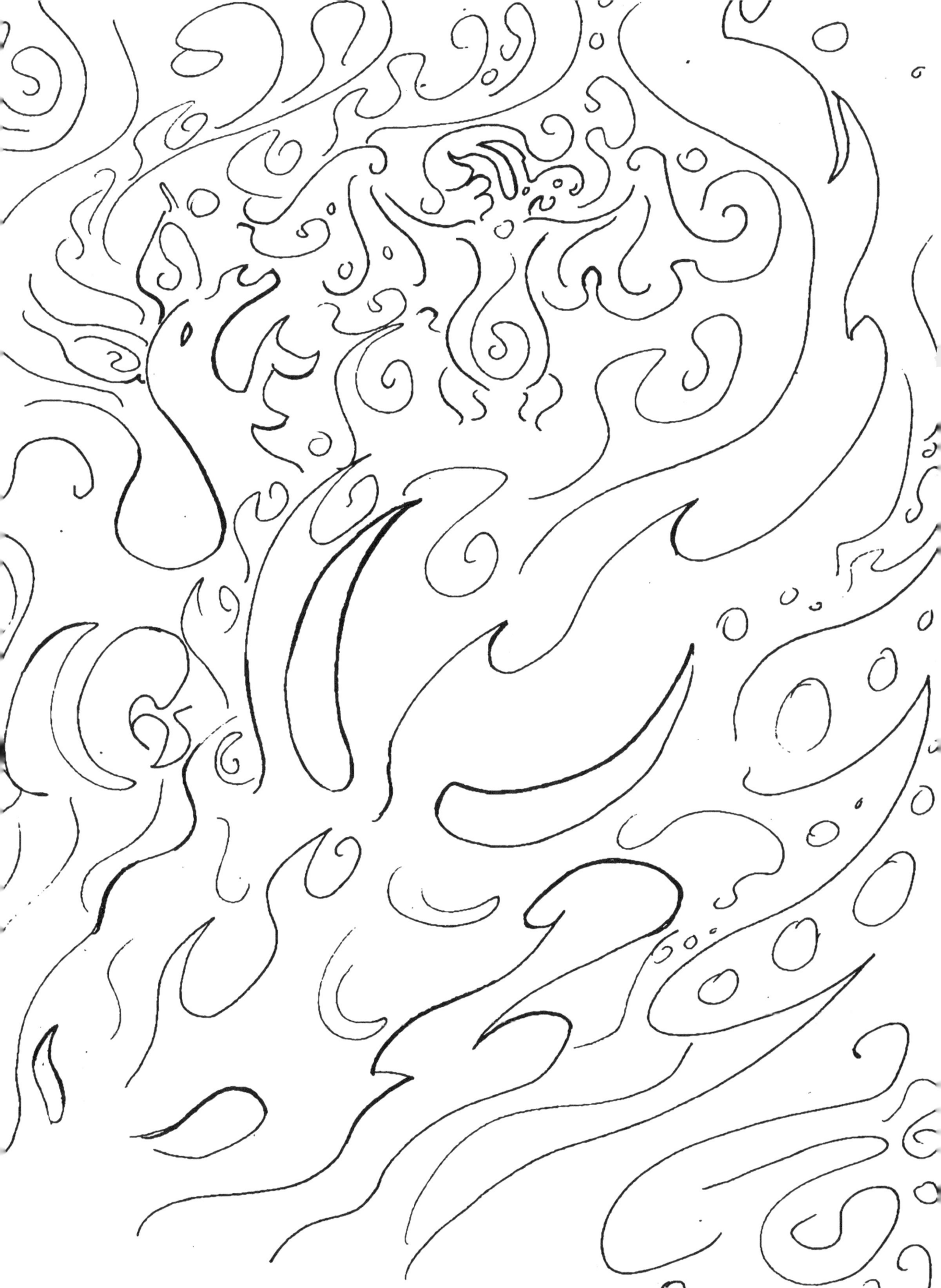

This page was left intentionally blank

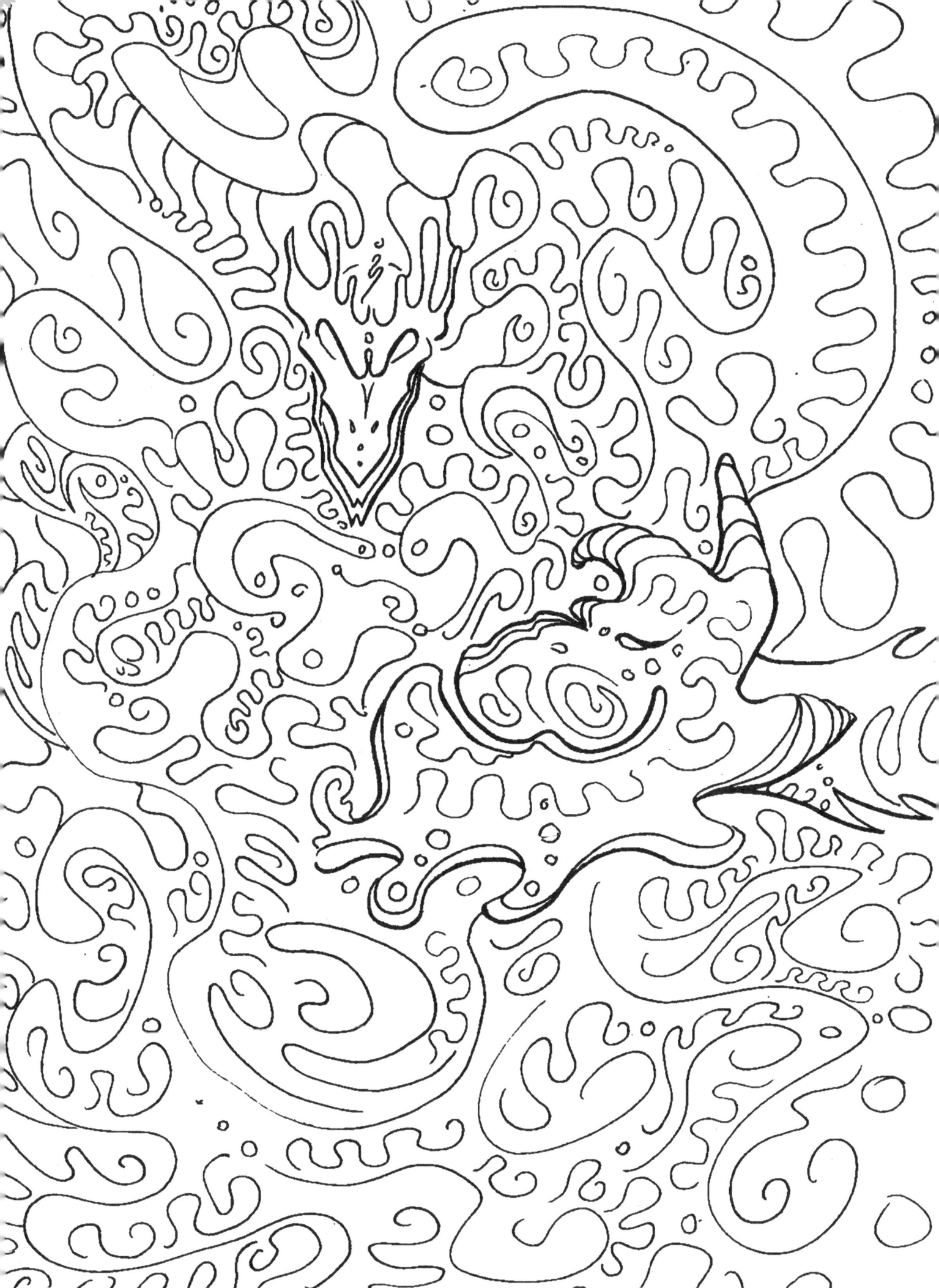

This page was left intentionally blank

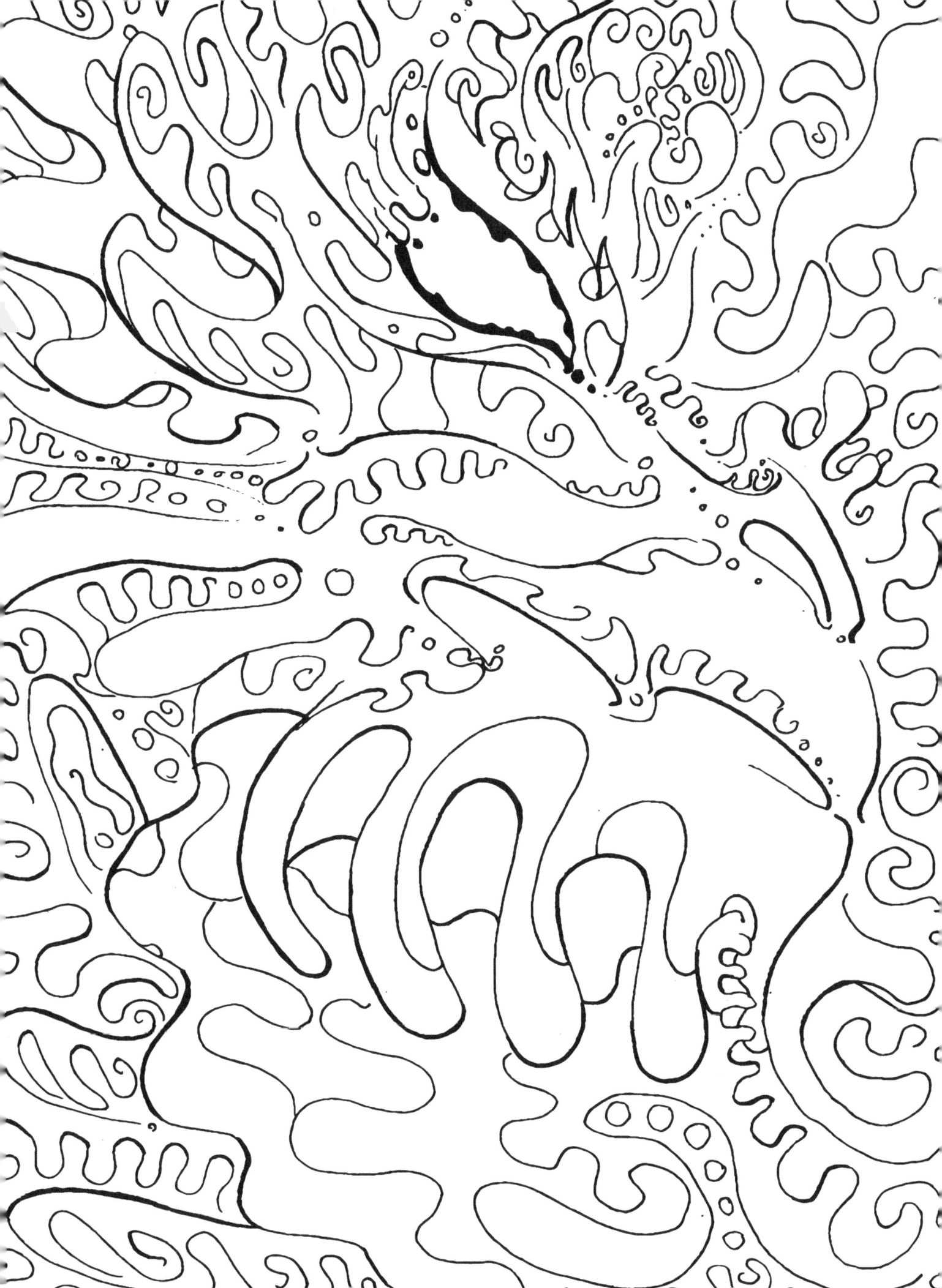

This page was left intentionally blank

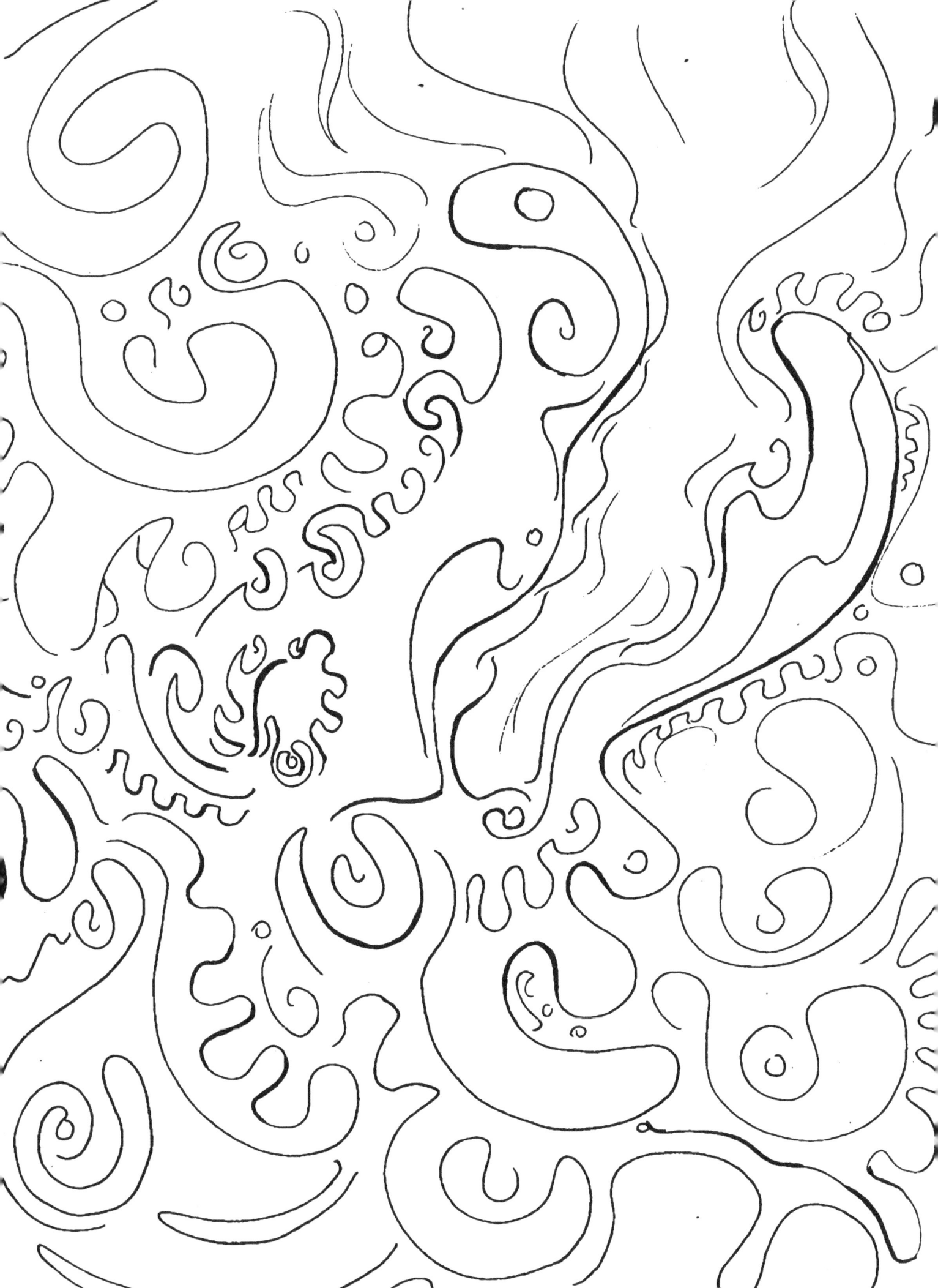

This page was left intentionally blank

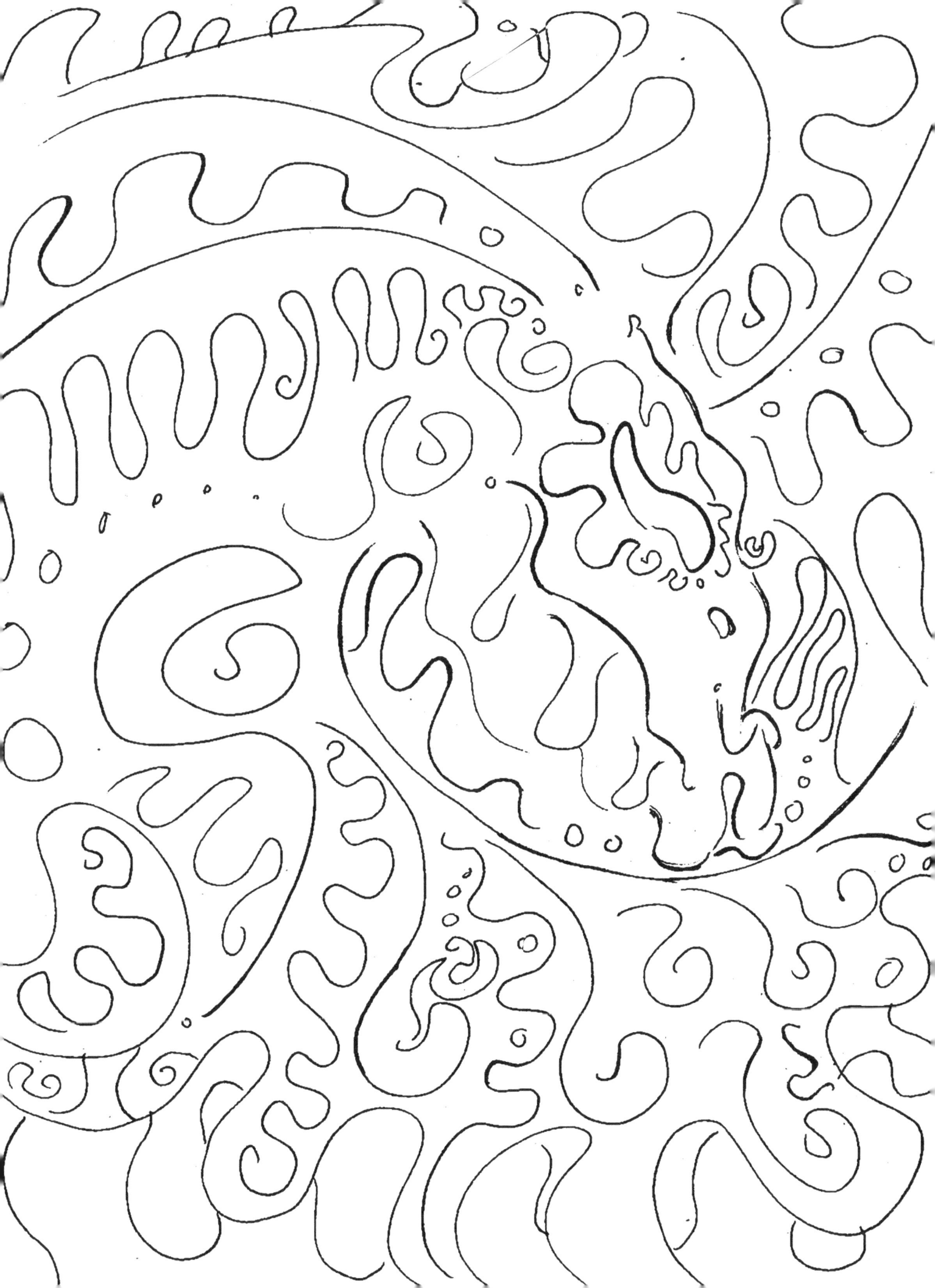

This page was left intentionally blank

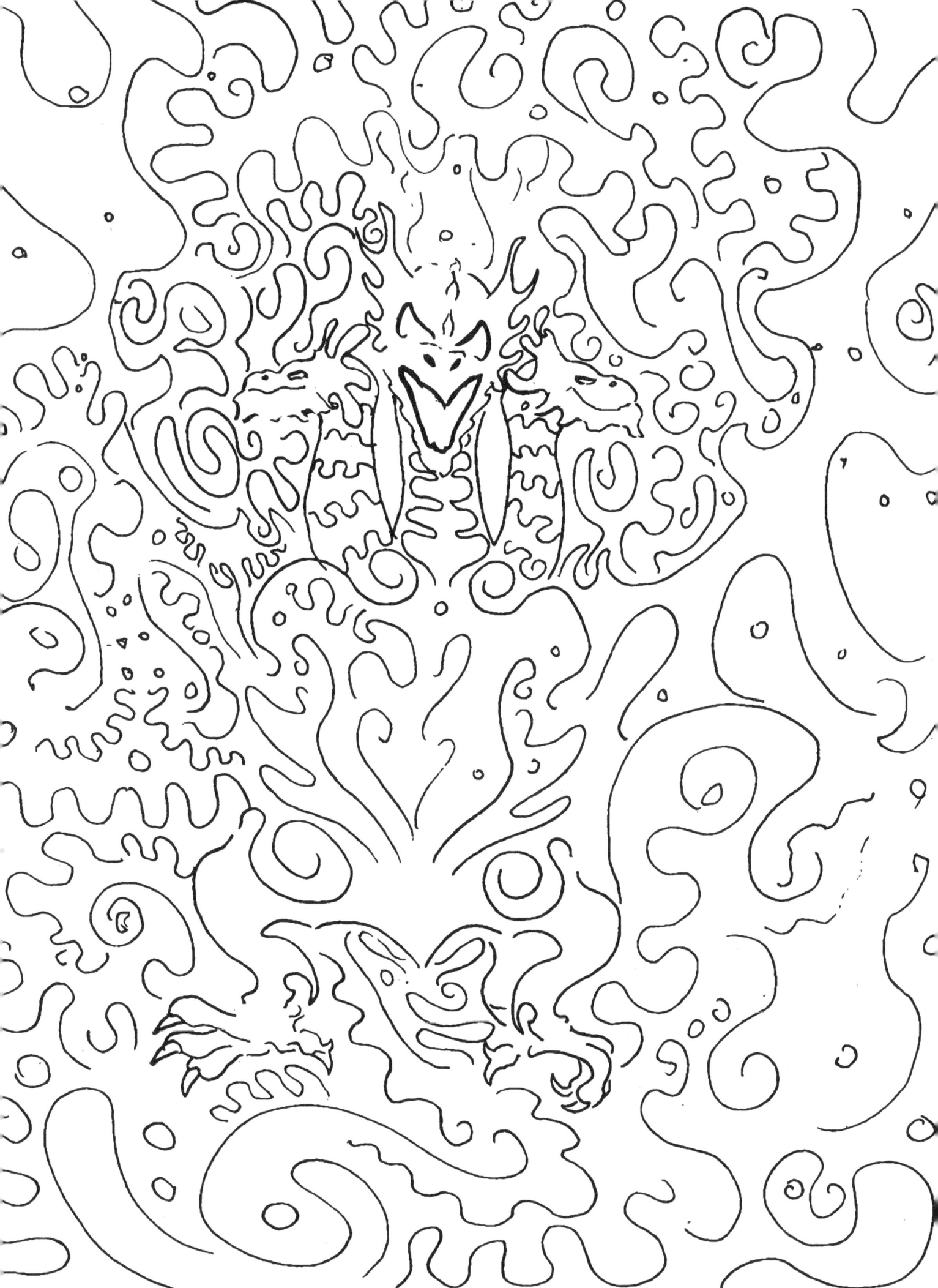

This page was left intentionally blank

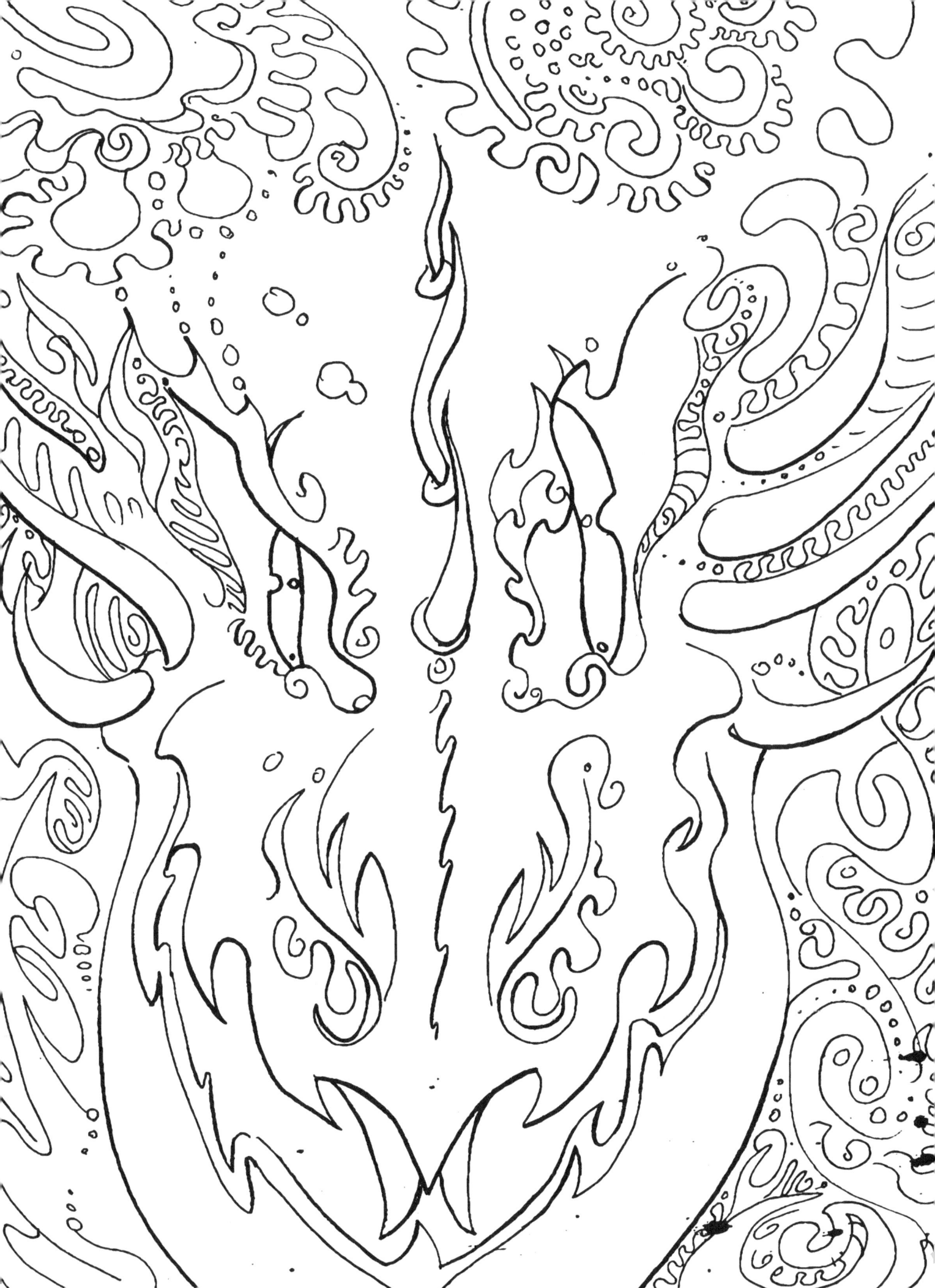

This page was left intentionally blank

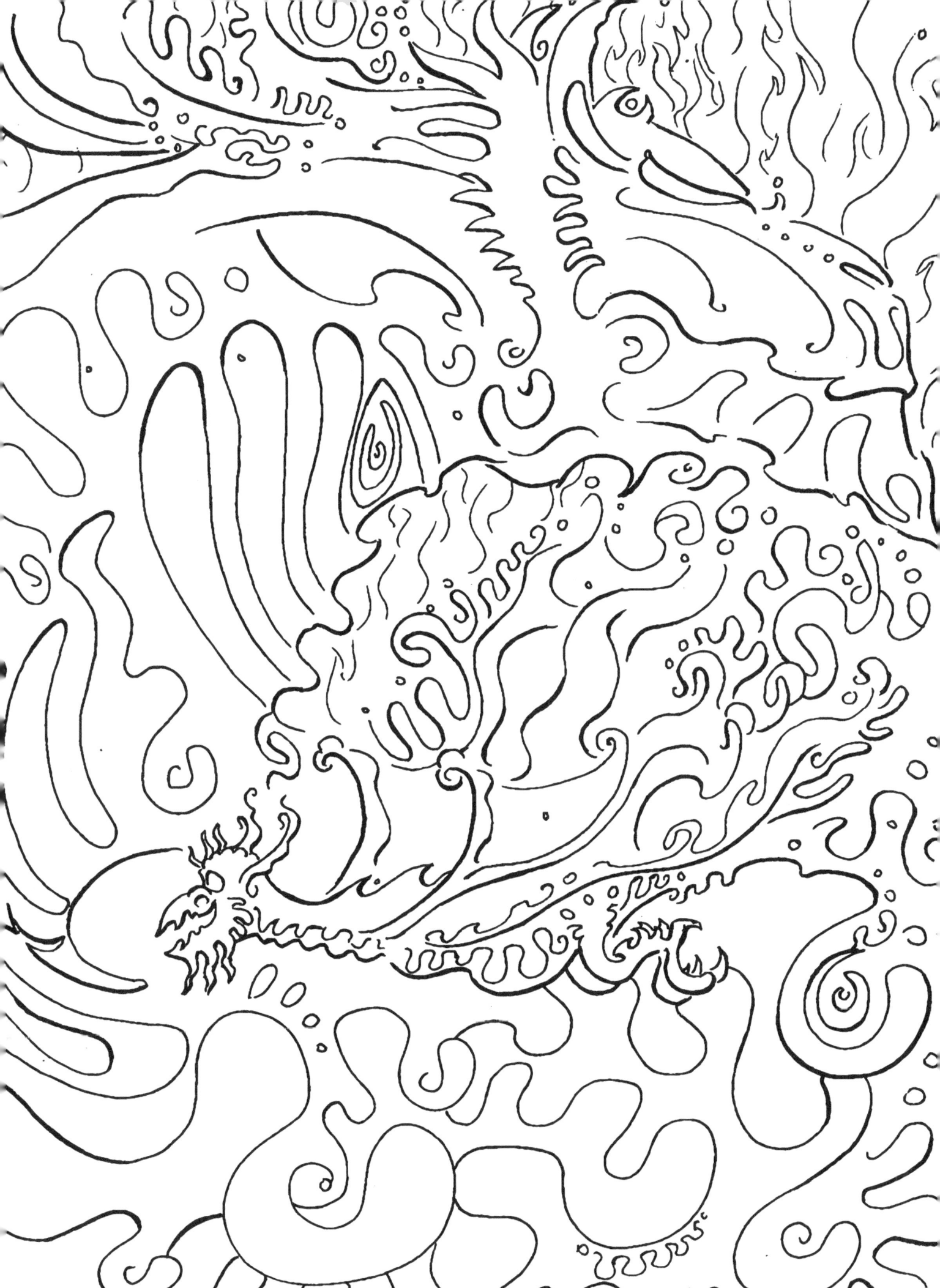

This page was left intentionally blank